God's Soul Desire

*Capturing God's heart
to reach the world He loves*

Daniel Bernard

Sovereign World

Sovereign World Ltd
PO Box 777
Tonbridge
Kent TN11 0ZS
England

Unless otherwise stated, all Scripture quotations are taken from the New
King James Version copyright © 1980 Thomas Nelson, Inc.

ISBN 1 85240 305 5

The publishers aim to produce books which will help to extend and
build up the Kingdom of God. We do not necessarily agree with every
view expressed by the author, or with every interpretation of Scripture
expressed. We expect each reader to make his/her judgement in the
light of their own understanding of God's Word and in an attitude of
Christian love and fellowship.

Typeset by CRB Associates, Reepham, Norfolk.
Printed in the United States of America

Contents

What Others Are Saying About
God's Soul Desire

'*God's Soul Desire* opens the Word of God and reminds us of the Lord's heart for the lost all around us. Dan Bernard has provided a stirring message for keeping our lives focused on sharing the gospel of our Lord Jesus Christ.'   ***Dr Pat Robertson***
Chairman and CEO, The Christian Broadcasting Network Inc.

'It is refreshing to meet someone with one burning passion that never abates. Dan Bernard has such a fervency to reach the lost and it is reflected in this book. I know that as you read it, you too will be ignited to seek and save the lost.'   ***Dr Terry Tekyl***
Founder, Renewal Ministries

'I highly recommend Dan Bernard's book. *God's Soul Desire* gives a challenge to each of us. In the same manner as the motto of our ministry, Dan shares a call to Consecration, Commitment and Action.'   ***Doug Stringer***
Founder, Turning Point Ministries

'*God's Soul Desire* is not just another book about evangelism. It is graphically illustrated and filled with inspirational and motivational reading, yet has enough "word" for pastors and leaders to use it as a training manual. I believe this book is very timely for the body of Christ today.'   ***Sandy Carson***
Founder, Prepare Ye The Way Ministries

'Few in Christ's Church have the zeal for the lost which Dan Bernard possesses. This book will raise up laborers within the body of Christ to do the will of God in these closing hours of time.'   ***Ray Comfort***
Founder, Living Waters Ministries

'As prayer has prepared the way for a tremendous worldwide harvest, so God is raising up the harvesters. Dan Bernard's book will help us to take that harvest. His passion for souls comes through on every page.'
Jerry Brandt
President, Action Evangelism & Project Light International

'*God's Soul Desire* is a refreshing look at evangelism. It dispels the "fear factor" and shows the awesome privilege and joy we have in preparing a bride for Christ's return. It shows a pure motivation for sharing the gospel that is compelling. If you too long to bring joy to the heart of God, this is the book for you!'
Jodie Nelson
Director of Outreach, Operation Blessing International

'*God's Soul Desire* will inspire the soul-winner in you! The powerful insights that are expressed in every chapter will reconfirm your position as a child of God, and the magnitude of the power that has been given you through His glory. This book will help to build your boldness for winning a lost generation and to execute the plan of God for your life.'
Dr Randy White
Senior Pastor, Without Walls International Church, Tampa, Florida

'*God's Soul Desire* is one of the best books on "why" we should witness for our Savior, Jesus. It gives a solid and clear message on how we can expand heaven's population with new souls. This is a must-read for people who want to win others to Christ.'
Paul Ridgeway
President, Ridgeway International

'Dan Bernard has a heart "for" God, and in an excellent way shows the servant attitude of a heart "to" God, in preparation for winning souls by the Holy Spirit. So, what would you attempt for God if you knew you could not fail?'
Frank W. Moseley
President, SOS International Spiritual Headquarters

'This is a simple, powerful book that speaks not only to the head, but to the heart. Dan Bernard understands that biblical evangelism is not merely human effort, but rather the ministry of the Holy Spirit through people who are yielded and available to be used by Him! To be effective witnesses for Jesus, we need to be more and more like Jesus!'
Paul Cedar
Chairman, Mission America

'*God's Soul Desire* will stir you to love people into the kingdom. If you're not motivated to share your love for Jesus with others, get ready for a spiritual heart transplant as you read this book.'
Peter Lowe
Founder, Success Events International

Foreword

I know thousands of people who are involved in ministry, but not many who cause me to bring a pen and paper along when I meet with them. When I get around Dan Bernard I bring my notebook because I know I will be learning new things about how to export the love of God in practical ways.

Undergirding Dan's life, ministry, and this new book *God's Soul Desire* are several vital lessons:

1. **Sow a lot of seeds of God's love.** All evangelism is good evangelism. Dan is an instigator of all sorts of evangelism approaches. He isn't necessarily committed to a single approach to sharing God's love, he is simply committed to loving people in a spectacular way, no matter what that looks like.

2. **Faithfulness pays off in the long run.** While it may take a while to get a ministry launched, hanging in there pays off if you go the distance with consistency. Dan likes to say, 'It takes a small thing done with great love to change Tampa Bay.' Lord, give me that sort of commitment!

3. **It doesn't take many resources to begin to make a difference.** Dan knows how to make much with little. That's my kind of guy – my kind of leader. I am hearing reports from church planters that they need a minimum of $100,000 in cash before they can begin to start a new congregation. Don't waste your time by trying to convince Dan with that sort of 'wisdom'. With few resources and little that is ideal, Dan can show you literally how to change your world.

4. **To do so is better than to say so.** Dan does what he talks about. It's not enough to have great-sounding theories about how things ought to work. The culture we live in right now is unwilling to tolerate much talk with little action.

Thanks, Dan, for writing this book. Thanks even more for living out a life that is worth following after.

Steve Sjogren
Founding Pastor, Vineyard Community Church
Cincinnati, Ohio, USA

Preface

This is not a 'how to' book on evangelism. There are many books on evangelism that give good insight and practical guidelines, but simply knowing the 'how to' without a heart for God is like someone giving you a driver's manual for a car that has no engine. Though I give practical instruction in this book, above all my hope is that the heart of God and what should be the heart of the Church would be imparted to you.

My approach will be to examine the story in Genesis 24 of Abraham's servant going to find a bride for Isaac and, as I do this, I ask that you keep in mind that there are several ways in which we can read and apply God's Word. We can read it subjectively, contextually, literally, and figuratively. I look at this account figuratively, believing that many events in the Old Testament are shadows of the reality found in the New Testament and also speak figuratively to us today.

I believe that Genesis 24 depicts God's desire to have His bride. In this allegorical story Abraham represents God the Father, in that he is served and respected. Isaac represents the Son of God, Jesus Christ; He is the one who is waiting for His bride and for prophecy to be fulfilled. The servant represents the work of the Holy Spirit through His Church to bring home the bride.

As I focus on the servant's relationship, character and consequent actions in achieving his assignment of retrieving a mate for the master's son, you will gain insight and instruction as an individual and as a member of the corporate body of Christ. You will discover what you and the Church are to be and do in accomplishing the mission of bringing home God's beloved wife. By the grace of the Holy Spirit you will receive the passion and the power to bring home His end-time bride.

I recommend that you familiarise yourself with the account by reading Genesis 24. It will also be helpful to read Isaiah 62 which parallels this passage. I pray God's blessings upon you as you read.

Introduction: Perspective

Do you recognise yourself in any of the following statements?

- When you were first converted, your witness was spontaneous and bold, but now it has waned, and you need encouragement to recover your first love.

- While you were in the evangelism program, you were on fire for God, but since its conclusion your witness has fizzled.

- You attend a congregation that started evangelism campaigns but, a year later, evangelism is non-existent and everyone wonders what has happened.

- You need to know what God wants and has wanted since the beginning of time.

Many start out as new Christians full of love and passion for Jesus, but, for one reason or another, become sidetracked or disillusioned. I hope reading this book will rekindle your desire to be a testimony to God's love. Above all else this book will give you God's perspective. And it is God's perspective we all need to keep the evangelism fires burning within us.

For an illustration of what I mean by perspective we can take the example of our cities' congested traffic. A reporter circling the city in a helicopter has a vantage point that the driver sitting in his car does not have and relays to the listening audience where the traffic jams are and how to avoid them. With this perspective he can avoid being delayed or immobilised by the heavy traffic. With God's perspective, we can keep from being immobilised in our witness.

The church often gets caught up in programs and activities that have nothing to do with its vision. We get busy with our own lives, in our daily routines, and forget our purpose. We often lose sight of why God has placed us in a particular job, neighborhood, or even on the face of the earth.

Another word for perspective is 'vision'. The Bible says,

> *'Where there is no vision, the people perish.'*
>
> (Proverbs 29:18)

The word 'perish' literally means to waste away. Without a vision God's people waste their time, their energy, and their talent. Something may appear to be fulfilling a godly purpose, yet in reality it does not serve God's ultimate purpose. Where the church is without a vision the lost perish.

Canon Theodore Wedel illustrates this point in the modern-day parable 'A Dangerous Seacoast':

> 'Volunteers from a nearby fishing village again and again braved the storm and rescued many from drowning, and those who were saved often joined the rescue corps.
>
> One day a volunteer suggested that with practice they could do an even better job. So in summer the rescue crews practiced rowing and throwing life preservers and were later able to save more lives. Another volunteer thought they should build a boathouse near the coast to keep the rescue boats. That way they would not waste time bringing their boats from the village. After a time, a third volunteer suggested that they build a shelter for the people they rescued, for they often died of the cold. And another recommended adding a kitchen to make soup to warm the storm victims. All these innovations added to the effectiveness of their work.
>
> Later a rescuer suggested that they wait in the boathouse during the storms so that they would be ready when a ship was wrecked. Another proposed adding a games room so that they would not be bored, and a

third that they expand the kitchen so that they would have hot drinks and food while they waited in the boathouse. The members took great pleasure in their building projects and added a lounge and a fine restaurant. The rescue station grew in prestige, and many more joined it on that account.

As time passed, one member observed that rescuing was a highly specialized task and that only those highly trained for it should be allowed to do the job. So they hired young men to go out in the storm while the rest cheered them on from the rescue complex. Finally the members had a meeting and decided to discontinue the lifesaving of the "club" altogether. It was too costly, and they all were too busy with related committee meetings and other activities.

A number protested that they had abandoned their primary purpose, so they resigned and started a real lifesaving station down the coast. Once again they went out into the storm and waves to rescue those who were drowning.

One day a volunteer suggested that with some practice they could do an even better job. So in the summer the rescue crews practiced rowing and throwing life preservers, and they rescued more people. Soon the crews from the club up the coast challenged them to a contest, for although the group had given up actual lifesaving, it retained "rescuing" as a summer sport. And when a rescue station won, its members were given a trophy to take home.

Later someone in the new group suggested that they build a boathouse near the coast to keep their boats, and another added that they needed a kitchen and shelter for those who were rescued. After a time, they added a games room and restaurant for those waiting on the coast during the storms.

Eventually, rescuing became a highly trained skill and specialists were hired to do the job. And one day the members decided to discontinue the lifesaving because it was costly and they were all busy. A number protested and moved down the coast to start a true rescue.'[1]

This parable paints an accurate picture of the Church throughout history. Believers who are on fire for Christ and saving those drowning in a sea of sin somehow get side-tracked into extracurricular activity which has nothing to do with rescuing the lost.

As believers, we should be saying, 'I don't want to waste anything. Let my life, all that I am, and all that I have count.' For this to happen, we need to ask God for His perspective, for His vision.

The Bible is a record of what God wants for His creation. One truth that stands out from Genesis to Revelation is that God wants to be in constant fellowship with His people. It was not good for man to be alone. Why? Human beings created in God's image have a need and desire for fellowship. God is self-sufficient. He, as the Father, Son and Holy Spirit, has sufficient fellowship. Therefore, He does not need our fellowship, but He **wants** our fellowship. God expresses His desire to have communion and fellowship with His creation by using the analogy of a bridegroom and bride – the most intimate relationship on the earth.

Throughout the Old Testament Scripture speaks of Israel being the bride of God. Israel was called to be a holy bride that would reveal the one true God to the nations. But the Israelites prostituted themselves and chose to serve other gods. (See Isaiah 54:5, 6; 62:4, 5; Jeremiah 22; Ezekiel 16; 8:2, 16; and Hosea 2; 16:20; Song of Songs.) When Jesus – the Bridegroom – came, He came for His bride. He declared, '*I was not sent except to the lost sheep of the house of Israel*' (Matthew 15:24). Israel was the bride-to-be. The Messiah came to earth to call His people together but, instead of being joined with this Bridegroom, the Jews jilted Him, as Isaiah had prophe-sied, '*He is despised and rejected by men*' (Isaiah 53:3). John 1:11 concurs, '*He came to His own, and His own did not receive Him.*' He came for His bride, but could not be united with her. Being a jealous bridegroom Jesus wanted a people solely for Himself. Through the parables Jesus explained that the kingdom was now being given over to the Gentiles. Jesus, the jealous bridegroom, jealous to have a people, jealous to have a bride, paid the debt for the sin of humankind by His death on the cross so that He could have a bride – the Church.

'Christ ... loved the church and gave Himself for her.'
(Ephesians 5:25)

Peter declared that now those *'who once were not a people ... are now the people of God'* (1 Peter 2:10). We have become the people of God. We have become the bride of Christ. We can look forward to a wedding day when the marriage will be consummated. From Genesis to Revelation we discover that what God wants is a bride – a people that will love Him as He loves them. No one sums it up better than the late Paul Billheimer in his book, *Destined for the Throne*:

> 'The final and ultimate outcome and goal of events from eternity to eternity, the finished product of all the ages, is the spotless Bride of Christ, united with Him in wedded bliss at the Marriage Supper of the Lamb and seated with her heavenly Bridegroom upon the throne of the universe – ruling and reigning with Him over an ever increasing and expanding Kingdom. He entered the stream of human history for this one purpose, to claim His Beloved (Revelation 19:6, 9; 21:7, 9, 10).
>
> Thus the Church, and only the Church, is the key to and explanation of history. The Church, blood-washed and spotless, is the center, the reason, and the goal of all of God's vast creative handiwork. Therefore, history is only the handmaiden of the Church, and the nations of the world are but puppets manipulated by God for the purposes of His Church (Acts 17:26). Creation has no other aim. History has no other goal. From before the foundation of the world until the dawn of eternal ages God has been working toward one grand event, one supreme end – the glorious wedding of His Son, the Marriage Supper of the Lamb.'[2]

That is God's soul desire. Therefore, those who are part of that bride, have the very heart of the Bridegroom. Those who have His heart know what He wants. They have His perspective and act upon it by going out to claim more people to make up His bride. This is our calling as the Church. This is why we exist. This is why we are the bride of Christ.

Study questions

1. Of the four opening statements, which one most describes you?

2. Do you feel that as God's highest creation you are fulfilling His ultimate purpose for your life? Why or why not?

3. In your own words explain God's ultimate purpose for His creation.

4. On a scale from 1 to 10 (10 being the highest), evaluate your prayer life and your witness for the Lord.

5. Do you believe the parable 'A Dangerous Seacoast' is an accurate portrayal of the Church? Where would you fit into this parable?

Notes

1. George E. Sweazy, 'Hiding From God Behind Religion,' in *Presbyterian Life* (1 September 1968).
2. Paul Billheimer, *Destined for the Throne* (Minneapolis: Bethany House, 1975), pp. 25–26.

Chapter 1

A Servant's Perspective:
A Present View from the Past

'Now Abraham was old, well advanced in age;
and the LORD *had blessed Abraham in all things.*
So Abraham said to the oldest servant of his house,
who ruled over all that he had . . . '
(Genesis 24:1, 2)

As I explained in the Preface, through the course of this book I look at Genesis 24 figuratively. In this account of a servant sent out to find a bride for his master's son, Abraham, the master, represents God the Father; Isaac, the son, represents the Son of God, Jesus Christ; and the servant, Eliezer, represents the work of the Holy Spirit through His Church.

Over many years Abraham's servant had developed a deep relationship with Abraham and Isaac, and it was this relationship that gave him a perspective on the awesome importance and responsibility of obtaining a bride for Isaac. He gained this perspective from a relationship. This is important for us: we too will gain the heart to win a bride for Christ from our relationship with God the Father and Son.

'Now Abraham was old, well advanced in age' (Genesis 24:1). Abraham was nearing the end of his life; his wife, Sarah, had already died. Eliezer had grown up in Abraham's household and served him for many years. It is evident from Abraham's prayer in Genesis 15:3, when he said *'one born in my house is my heir'*, that, until the birth of Isaac, Abraham had counted

him as his heir: he was like a son to him. Eliezer had seen
Abraham leave everything to fulfill the promise that God
had given him – to become the father of many nations
(Genesis 12). Over the years he had witnessed Abraham
suffer, struggle, and fail.

When the fulfillment of the promise was delayed, Abraham had begun to take the matter into his own hands.
Thinking the promise would be fulfilled through Eliezer, he
attempted to adopt him as his son but the word of the Lord
came to him saying, *'This one shall not be your heir, but one
who will come from your own body...'* (Genesis 15:4). Despite
the fact that Sarah was beyond childbearing years, the child
was to come from Abraham's seed. Sarah, assuming that her
younger maidservant Hagar was to bear the child, directed
Abraham to marry her and through Hagar Abraham had a
son called Ishmael. But Ishmael was not to be the son of
promise (Genesis 17:21).

Finally, when 99-year-old Abraham had given up all hope
that the promise would be fulfilled, three angels came to tell
him that within a year he would have a child. As the angels
foretold, a year later the child was born and was named Isaac.
As the child grew, the promise seemed secure, until one day
when God told Abraham to take Isaac up on the mountain
and sacrifice him. Eliezer saw Abraham struggle with the
prospect of sacrificing Isaac. But the Bible tells us that
Abraham reasoned within himself that even if he were to
sacrifice his son, God had the power to raise him back up
again (Hebrews 11:17–19), and so he raised his knife to
plunge it into the heart of his one and only son. Providentially, an angel stopped him and Jehovah God provided
another sacrifice. Despite overcoming these many trials, if
God's promise to Abraham was to be fulfilled, Isaac needed a
bride, and Eliezer understood this.

Although it would be wrong to push the analogy too far,
there are many parallels between Abraham's life story and
God's plan for the final chapter of history. As we read and
study God's Word, and begin to understand God's struggles
to have a bride, we begin to gain His perspective. We learn
about His dealings with the obstinate people of Israel; we
learn about the sacrifice of God the Son coming to earth,

battling in the Garden of Gethsemane and sweating blood as He prayed; we see Him humiliated, ridiculed, spat upon, literally mutilated as He was beaten beyond recognition; we see Him suffering, dying, rising again and ascending into heaven: all to win His bride. We understand that on the day of Pentecost God brought His Church into being in glory and power. But then came the downward spiral as the Church entered the dark ages and became embroiled in religion and ritual all over again, as it lost perspective and the power of the Holy Spirit.

Throughout church history, God has continued to work with His people in order to have a bride. He raised up men like Luther to bring about the Reformation, and others like Calvin, Zwingli, Knox, Huss, Zinzendorf, Wesley, Finney and Moody to purify the Church and redirect it towards the goal of making His bride ready for the Bridegroom. Today, as we enter the last days, we see God continuing to grapple to this end. He grieves over the Church's divisions, doctrinal wars, heresies and heretics.

Abraham's servant was an eyewitness of his master's past struggles. Through them, he gained the perspective of the present need to bring home a bride. In the same way, the past gives us the proper perspective of the present need. Abraham was old and his wife was dead (Genesis 24:1). There was no chance of another child. The promise Abraham had lived for was yet to be fulfilled. Everything hinged on Isaac getting a bride. It was up to the servant to do it. What a responsibility! What a privilege! Today's servant Church is in the last days of the earth's existence. Time is running out. The Bridegroom is about to descend from heaven to take His bride home. Yet, at least 2.5 billion people are without a living witness of Jesus Christ among them, and many more are without a saving relationship with Him.

Keith Green once said, 'This present generation of Christians is responsible for the next generation of Christians.' Every generation must obey the call of the Lord Jesus Christ to fulfill the Great Commission in their lifetime. We must bring home the bride. Once we know the past struggles of God the Father and Son, not to involve ourselves in the desire of their hearts can only be viewed as callous, careless and sinful. Like Abraham commissioning his servant, God has no other plan to get a bride. He plans to use you, His servant, to meet the present need. It is an awesome privilege and responsibility. You and I have the honor of bringing home the bride for our Lord Jesus Christ.

Knowing the past struggle (it is important to know church history, as it gives us perspective) and knowing the future fulfillment of the promise makes the present need especially great. The laborers are still few. There is nothing more important. The great men and women of the past knew this and their lives give us perspective on the grave responsibility and privilege that we have to bring home a bride.

William McDonald in his book, *True Discipleship*, tells how one great man viewed this responsibility and privilege. He relates how President Coolidge asked John Mott, a well-known missionary-statesman, to serve as ambassador to Japan. Mott replied to him, 'Mr President, since God called me to be an ambassador of His, my ears have been deaf to all other calls.' [1]

Billy Graham also tells the story of a missionary with a higher calling:

> 'When the Standard Oil Company was looking in the Far East for a man, they chose a missionary to be their representative. They offered him ten thousand, and he turned it down; twenty-five thousand, and he turned it down; fifty thousand, and he turned it down. They said, "What's wrong?" He said, "Your price is all right, but your job is too small."' [2]

The job of bringing home a bride for the Lord Jesus Christ is the most privileged and fulfilling. It is an assignment whose eternal significance and rewards outweigh those of presidents and kings. The servant was invaluable to Abraham; his worth was priceless.

Luke 5:10 says, '...*From now on you will catch men.*' The word 'catch' is ζωγρεω (dzogue-reh'-o) in the Greek (this word only occurs on one other occasion in the New Testament). It means to snare or to take alive like one catching fish in a net. In 2 Timothy 2:26, Paul exhorts Timothy to instruct gently people who have fallen so that they may *'escape the **snare** of the devil.'* Satan also wants to snare people. But where Satan wants to bring people to death and destruction, God wants to take men and women alive. Therefore, we must take them alive! Not only so that people will escape hell fire, but because living human beings are valuable to God.

God works through human beings; **we** are the agents that God uses. Angels do not preach the gospel. The angel told Peter to go to the Gentile, Cornelius, who was seeking God (Acts 10:17ff.). Angels could have done it, but God uses people. E.M. Bounds agrees:

> 'When God declares that "the eyes of the Lord run to and fro throughout the whole earth, to shew himself strong in the behalf of them whose heart is perfect towards him" (2 Chronicles 16:9), He declares the necessity of men. He acknowledges His dependence on them as a channel through which He can exert His power on the world.'[3]

Of course, it is through the same humankind that Satan will yield his kingdom of darkness. Therefore, we must take people alive. Men and women are valuable to God.

We can see how precious we are to God as His children in a passage that parallels Genesis 24:

> *'¹For Zion's sake I will not hold My peace,*
> *And for Jerusalem's sake I will not rest,*
> *Until her righteousness goes forth as brightness,*
> *And her salvation as a lamp that burns.*
> *²The Gentiles shall see your righteousness,*
> *And all kings your glory.*
> *You shall be called by a new name,*
> *Which the mouth of the* LORD *will name.*
> *³You shall also be a crown of glory*
> *In the hand of the* LORD,
> *And a royal diadem*
> *In the hand of your God.*
> *⁴You shall no longer be termed Forsaken,*
> *Nor shall your land any more be termed Desolate;*

But you shall be called Hephzibah, and your land Beulah;
For the Lord *delights in you,*
And your land shall be married.
⁵For as a young man marries a virgin,
So shall your sons marry you;
And as the bridegroom rejoices over the bride,
So shall your God rejoice over you.'   (Isaiah 62:1–5)

Note, in verse 3, how God views those who arise and shine and take salvation to the nations: *'You shall also be a crown of glory in the hand of the* Lord.*'* In other words, you are precious to the Lord. God cares about you very much. He is personally going to keep you. The nations will see your righteousness and all kings see your glory. You will be called by a new name that the mouth of the Lord will bestow (v. 4). No longer are you useless and unproductive. God delights in you. He is personally involved and concerned with your welfare and wants to protect and keep you as His own.

To really get the full understanding of Isaiah 62:5, it is helpful to examine the New Testament parallel spoken by Jesus in Luke 15:10:

' . . . there is joy |or rejoicing| *in the presence of the angels of God over one sinner who repents.'*

Note who is doing the rejoicing. It is not the angels (although I am sure they are rejoicing), but there is rejoicing in the midst of the angels. Who is in the middle of the angels? Jesus! The Bible tells us, *'angels stood around the throne'* (Revelation 7:11) and *' . . . the Lamb . . . is in the midst of the throne'* (Revelation 7:17). My God, Jesus, King of kings, Creator . . . rejoices over you and each sinner who repents. Does it not excite you to know that you can cause God to stand up and shout by bringing one person to Christ!

The servant Eliezer is successful. He brings home a bride for the father and son. Imagine a frail, toothless Abraham saying 'Well done, faithful servant.' Imagine the rejoicing as the promise is fulfilled.

One day, we will actually have such an experience, but on a much grander scale. We will see the joy on the face of our

Bridegroom who has waited for the arrival of His bride. He will rejoice over you, not only as part of His bride, but also as one who satisfied His soul desire by bringing home the bride. Now, that is perspective.

Study questions

1. Do you feel you have God's perspective? What is the key to gaining God's perspective?

2. Give an example of how having the right or wrong perspective has helped or hurt you.

3. The servant's relationship with Abraham gave him a unique perspective of the significance of the bride. How has your relationship with the Father affected your perspective?

4. Keith Green said, 'This present generation of Christians is responsible for the next generation of Christians.' Do you feel you are personally responsible? Explain.

5. How should biblical history shape our present perspective and consequent action?

6. How are you affected by the idea that the highest calling on earth is being God's ambassador? Does it affect the way you think and act daily?

7. According to the latter part of the chapter, God sees you as invaluable. List other examples of how God sees you.

8. This week meditate on Isaiah 62:5 and Luke 15:10. How is your outlook on evangelism affected by the fact that Jesus rejoices over you?

Notes

1. William McDonald, *True Discipleship* (Benin City: Maranatha, 1963), p. 65.

2. Charles G. Trumball, *Taking Men Alive* (London: Letterworth Press, 1957), p. 7.

3. E.M. Bounds, *Power through Prayer* (Springdale: Whitaker House, 1982), p. 8.

Chapter 2

The Relationship:
Master to Servant

*'So Abraham said to the **oldest servant of his house**...'*
(Genesis 24:2)

My wife, Kathy, and I have been married since 1982. Together we attended seminary, pastored two churches, evangelised in a street ministry, have been missionaries to Nigeria, W. Africa, and are currently doing city-reaching in the Tampa Bay area through *Somebody Cares Tampa Bay*. Also, by God's grace, we have brought our children, Leah, Luke, Bethany, Faith, Peter and Rachel into this world.

We have had our highs and lows, our failures and victories; we have prayed, cried, laughed, and sung together numerous times. Through these experiences we have formed a deep relationship. If you were to ask me about Kathy, I would tell you about her; but not because I went to seminary or read a book that gives general information on women or wives. I would tell you the things you wanted to know about Kathy because I know her from experience. I live and communicate with her on a daily basis. I know her ins and outs, her plans, her hopes, her fears. I know everything about my wife and I can tell you instantly what you need to know.

This is how we tell others about Jesus Christ. This is evangelism. I cannot tell you about God unless I know Him. I cannot get others to put their trust in Him if I have not learned to trust Him myself. I must know God to make Him known. I cannot give to someone else what I do not have. Becoming a Christian is getting to know the person of Christ, not a creed or set of religious dogmas. It is impossible to evangelise without a relationship with God the Father. The very core of evangelism is revealing God to a lost and dying world. To glorify God is to reveal Him as He is.

When we think of evangelism, we tend to picture some wide-eyed zealous new convert, bursting with joy. Those who have just found Jesus have a testimony and a relationship with Him, but do not know God to the same degree as the person who has walked by the Spirit for many years. The new convert cannot reveal the very character and personhood of God in the same way as one who is older in the faith. Daniel 11:32 states, *'but the people who know their God shall be strong and carry out great exploits.'* Who really knows God: the new convert or the individual who has walked with God for ten or twenty years?

In Genesis 24:2, Abraham's servant is described as *'the oldest servant of his house,'* who *'...ruled over all that he* [Abraham] *had.'* His age and the fact he was made responsible for his master's belongings indicate that he was probably the most mature, faithful and loyal of Abraham's servants. These qualities came about through time spent with the man of God, Abraham. The older, mature believer who has demonstrated loyalty, faithfulness and commitment is the most qualified to do evangelism, as Eliezer was the most qualified to search for Isaac's bride.

The mature believer is more effective because he or she is a demonstration, not merely an explanation, of who God is. Who can demonstrate God better than the person who has spent years learning from Him, taking on His character and ministry? Unfortunately, we often find the very opposite in the church. Rather than the older people leading the way in evangelism, they often are a source of discouragement not only to the young convert but to anyone who desires to evangelise.

I remember being a new zealous convert. I was obnoxious for God, telling everyone about Jesus (whether they wanted to hear or not). The pillars of the church would say, 'Yes, we remember when we were like that. You take it easy. This zeal will wear off after a while and you will become like one of us.' Though I was overzealous and could have used more wisdom in my approach, I was genuinely excited about my newfound relationship with Jesus Christ.

The reality is that lost zeal is a reflection of a lost relationship. Keith Green wrote an article entitled 'Zeal: The Good, the Bad and the Ugly' in which he defined true zeal as 'directing all our energies and enthusiasm into our relationship with the Lord and then into our relationship with our neighbor.' [1] Jesus told us that the greatest commandment is to love the Lord with all your heart, mind and soul and strength and, the second greatest, to love your neighbor as yourself (Mark 12:30–31). True zeal for God is knowing Him enthusiastically and then, from the overflow of our relationship with Him, desiring God's vision to see the salvation of humankind. We must have a relationship with God in order to do the evangelistic work of revealing Him to the world.

There are four aspects to the relationship the servant, Eliezer, had with Abraham. They related as: master/servant; owner/steward; covenant partner, friend/friend; and father/son. I believe that these aspects mirror our relationship with God. But, before we begin to examine these different aspect, we must understand the fundamental truth that God has a greater relationship with us than we can ever have with Him. He is infinite and we are finite. What does this mean? It means He can be more to us than we can be to Him. As we look at these four aspects, in this and the next three chapters, we need to remember that our relationship to God is like the servant's relationship to Abraham.

First, let us look more closely at the master/servant aspect to their relationship. Romans 6:18 says,

> *'And having been set free from sin, you became slaves of righteousness.'*

We are born again, born in the Spirit, made free from sin through the blood of Jesus, to become servants of righteousness. As servants of righteousness, we have no rights. Our obedience is not optional. Evangelism is, therefore, not optional. The Great Commission is not optional. We obey our Master in just the same way that the servant obeyed Abraham. Going to get a bride was the servant's duty. No way

could the servant say, 'No, Abraham. I just do not feel led
today.' Bringing home a bride for the Lord Jesus Christ is our
duty.

Eliezer had been a servant for many years. It was the
practice in Old Testament times for servants, after seven
years of service, to be given the option to go free. But
sometimes the servant would choose to stay on in service
because of the goodness of his master. This practice became
part of the Levitical law:

> *'But if the servant plainly says, "I love my master, my wife,
> and my children; I will not go out free," then his master shall
> bring him to the door, or to the doorpost, and his master
> shall pierce his ear with an awl; and he shall serve him
> forever.'*   (Exodus 21:5, 6)

The piercing of the ear was a symbol of the servant's love and
loyalty towards his master and marked him as the master's
property. Such a servant became known as a free-will bondservant. I believe Eliezer became a free-will bondservant,
choosing to servant his master, Abraham.

'Bond-servant' is the word used in Romans 6:18, translated
in the New King James Version as 'slaves'. We become
bondservants or free-will servants when we choose to serve
God. We are marked with a spiritual awl. We are no longer
our own, but we were bought with a price. The price was the
precious blood of Jesus. We no longer belong to ourselves but
belong to Jesus Christ, our Lord and Master. It is our duty as
servants to obey what the Lord, our Master, has commanded:

> *'Go and make disciples of all nations . . .'*   (Matthew 28:19)

Note that this master/servant relationship is an intimate
one. It is out of free will that you say as the servant said, 'I
love my master.' You do not do His commands merely out of
duty. The bondservant loved his master, and I believe that
this love would have continued to grow as time went on. It is
the same with us.

In John 15, Jesus, in one of His last intimate conversations
with His disciples before going to the cross, says,

'No longer do I call you servants, for a servant does not know what his master is doing; but I have called you friends, for all things that I heard from My Father I have made known to you.' (John 15:16)

He no longer calls them servants but friends. Why? Because, having grown in their relationship together, He could share details with them He could only entrust to intimate friends. Jesus said in John 14:15:

'If you love me, keep my commandments.'

As servants we are motivated by our duty to obey, but as bondservants, in an intimate relationship, we are motivated by love for our master. We have a good Master who has set us free. He has set us free from slavery to Satan and to sin by His precious blood. We have become free-will bondservants to the will of God, to the will of His person and to the will of His working. Therefore, Jesus says, *'No longer do I call you servants ... but I have called you friends.'* We, as servants with love in our hearts, gladly fulfill the duty of bringing home the bride.

After Abraham's servant had sworn that he would take a wife for Isaac from the daughters of the Canaanites, he immediately set out to fulfill his promise. He asked the Lord to show him who the bride would be, praying very specifically. He prayed:

' "Behold, here I stand by the well of water, and the daughters of the men of the city are coming out to draw water. Now let it be that the young woman to whom I say, 'Please let down your pitcher that I may drink,' and she says, 'Drink, and I will also give your camels a drink' – let her be the one You have appointed for Your servant, Isaac. And by this I will know that You have shown kindness to my master." And it happened, before he had finished speaking, that behold, Rebekah, who was born to Bethuel, son of Milcah, the wife of Nahor, Abraham's brother, came out with her pitcher on her shoulder.'

(Genesis 24:13–15)

The servant prayed for a divine appointment with the right woman to wed Isaac. He had ten camels which had traveled hundreds of miles. The water gauge on these camels was on 'E' – **empty**! It was time to fill up. Eliezer stopped praying, looked up, saw a young woman, and approached her. Her response to his request was not only to offer water to Eliezer but to draw water for his camels as well. It takes about thirty gallons of water to fill up one camel.[2] She may have drawn 300 gallons of water out of the well. Now, that is servant-hood!

The bride of Christ is going to be a servant-bride. Notice that Eliezer did not pray that the prospective bride would be pretty or talented, but that she would have that unselfish character that comes with a servant's heart. I believe that what Eliezer prayed was the heart of Abraham. This is also what Jesus has told us to pray. He said:

> *'Therefore pray the Lord of the harvest to send out laborers into His harvest.'*   (Matthew 9:38)

The key to evangelism is not praying for the lost but praying for laborers for the ripened fields of souls. Jesus is looking for those who will serve Him out of love.

It is interesting that, although Genesis 24 does not specifically mention the servant's name, we assume him to be Eliezer who is mentioned in Genesis 15. This is the story of the nameless servant or the no-name servant. Eliezer does not receive the credit for bringing home the bride, although we can assume that it was him. Someone once said that 'there's no telling how much could be done in the church if someone didn't have to get the credit.' I think God is going to write another book after Revelation is fulfilled and the world is over. It is going to be God's reflections on world history and it will be called, 'Nameless Servants: How the World was Won'.

God is mobilising average believers of all ages. The local church is becoming the training and sending base for everyday believers. The superstar mentality is dead. We can appreciate the great crusades and TV evangelists and the work they are doing, but the bottom line is that the world is going to be won by nameless bondservants that say, 'I love my Master and I will serve Him forever by bringing a bride home for His Son.'

The call to be the bride of Christ, to be the local church, is a call to endless servanthood. There are some things from which you never graduate in the body of Christ. One is servanthood. We are following the One who said,

> *'I did not come to be served but to serve and to give my life as a ransom for many.'*   (Mark 10:45)

Jesus, who first loved us by giving His life for us, compels and constrains us to be that servant, not just out of duty, but out of love for the One who set us free. Has His love pierced your heart to the extent where you are ready to become the free-will bondservant? Can you say, 'I love You, Lord. I want to bring home a bride for You,' and then go and do it?

Study questions

1. Without taking too much time to think about it, describe the personality of someone you know. (Usually, the more intimately we know someone, the more descriptive we will be.)

2. Again, without taking too much time to think about it, can you describe God and your relationship with Him to someone else. Write at least a paragraph.

3. Like Eliezer with Abraham, we have a master/servant relationship with God. How should this affect our response to the command our Master has given us regarding evangelising and discipling?

4. It is our duty as servants to obey the Great Commission. Yet, God desires that we fulfill this duty with love and joy in our hearts. Can you say, 'I love my Master. I will gladly take on the duty of bringing home a bride'? What has God done for you that would cause you to serve Him with love and joy?

5. From Eliezer's prayer, what can we discover that God is seeking in us? God has all the gifts and talents we will need ready to bestow upon us; therefore, He really does not need our gifts or talents. What is God really looking for in you?

6. How do you feel about being a lifetime servant of Christ, who may never receive any applause from your fellow human beings?

Notes

1. Keith Green, 'Zeal: The Good, The Bad, and The Ugly', *Last Days Magazine* 16 (March 1993), 22.

2. David S. Kirkwood, *Your Best Year Yet* (Lake Mary: Creation House, 1990), p. 27.

Chapter 3

The Relationship:
Owner to Steward

'So Abraham said to the oldest servant of his house,
who ruled over all that he had . . .'
(Genesis 24:2)

In Genesis 24:2 we see another aspect of the relationship between Abraham and his servant. Abraham was a wealthy man, richly blessed by God. He was the owner, yet he entrusted his servant with the stewardship of all that he owned. Jesus is our Lord and the owner of our very lives. He has this right to be our owner, above all, because He is the Creator and we are His creation (John 1:3; Psalms 24:1; 89:1).

The Bible says:

' . . . do you not know that . . . you are not your own? For you were bought at a price; therefore glorify God in your body.'
(1 Corinthians 6:19, 20)

You are not your own! All that you have, all that you are, all that you ever hope to be, as Dallas Holmes sings, is His. He owns it. Jesus Christ is the rightful owner because He has purchased the rights to our lives through His shed blood. He is your owner because He has redeemed you, or bought you back, from the devil. You were in the kingdom of darkness and through His blood you have been purchased and placed into the kingdom of light. He owns us and we are His stewards. When He purchased us, He invested in us His life, His Spirit, His grace, power and ability.

Genesis 1:28 tells us that human beings were created to have dominion and to rule over every living thing. In Genesis 3, however, Adam lost that dominion. By sinning, he gave it away to Satan. Every man and woman since Adam has also sinned and yielded his or her rights to Satan. Satan is the prince of this lost and sin-filled world. In Matthew 4, Satan came to Jesus and offered Him the kingdoms of the world if He would bow down to him. Jesus never refuted the fact that Satan had the authority to offer Him the kingdoms. Satan had that authority. Once we are redeemed in God, we become a second Adam through Jesus Christ. Like the first Adam, we are to take dominion and subdue the earth again. Our main means of subduing the earth and gaining dominion is through the preaching of the gospel of salvation. Jesus invested His life, Spirit, grace and power to enable us to live and witness. Many people coming to Christ will result in whole cultures and societies being redeemed through the gospel – the good news of Jesus Christ.

Francis Frangipane in his book, *The Three Battlegrounds*, tells how the gospel has changed the crime rate in Cedar Rapids, Iowa, by 17 per cent.[1] The earth is being subdued through the gospel. The history of missions is the transformation of people, groups and nations through the gospel. The gospel transforms us from poverty to production, from no antidote against lethal diseases to healings (medically and supernaturally), from anarchy to order and peace. Laws do not change governments because laws are kept and enforced by human beings. People need to be transformed by the power of the gospel before governments will change.

Saying that Jesus Christ has invested His life, power and grace in us as individuals and the corporate body of Christ is tantamount to saying that He has invested in His kingdom. He has given us the kingdom (Luke 12:32). We are commanded to establish the kingdom on the earth as we pray and preach (Matthew 6).

We are stewards of the kingdom of God. Jesus, in the parable of the unmerciful servant, speaks about accountability in and for His kingdom:

'Therefore the kingdom of heaven is like a certain king who wanted to settle accounts with his servants.'

(Matthew 18:23)

Stewardship is the use or oversight of that with which you have been entrusted. We express what our Master has deposited in our lives by depositing the kingdom in others. Out of gratitude in our hearts for the King and His everlasting kingdom, we work to establish His dominion in and through men and women's hearts. Phillips Steins writes about God's purpose in entrusting the kingdom to Israel:

'Israel also was established as a kingdom. The Davidic dynasty was to be the model of God's authorized presence with his people ... David well understood why God had called Israel. The kingdom was not an end in itself, but God's means to make His Name glorious among the nations (1 Chronicles 16:8, 24, 28; Psalms 67; 86:8–10; 96:3–10). Through the righteous rule of an earthly king, God would not only draw nations to Himself, but the message of His glory would be carried to the nations by His people through trade, state business, and ordinary encounters with peoples.

The kingdom was so significant that our Lord made it the theme of His earthly ministry. He compared Israel's stewardship of the kingdom to a vineyard which was to be kept for God's purposes, describing how, by default, the kingdom was taken away from those who had originally received it, and given to another who would return to Him its yield (Matthew 21:33–41). Immediately before His ascension, the kingdom was still the topic of discourse (Acts 1:6–7). The church has been entrusted with the same kingdom stewardship.'[2]

Israel was supposed to be a steward of God's kingdom, but when it failed in that stewardship, Jesus turned the kingdom over to the Gentiles, to you and me (Matthew 21:43). Now we are called the light and the salt of the earth. The means we use to fulfill this calling is the gospel.

The 'Parable of the Orange Tree', by Dr John White, depicts our responsibility as Christians and the consequences when we do not carry it out:

'I dreamed I drove on a Florida road, still and straight and empty. On either side were groves of orange trees ... This was harvest time. My wonder grew as the miles slipped by. How could the harvest be gathered?

... But at last I saw some orange pickers. Far from the highway, almost on the horizon, lost in the vast wilderness of unpicked fruit, I could discern a tiny group of them working steadily. And many miles later I saw another group. I could not be sure, but I suspected that the earth beneath me was shaking with silent laughter at the hopelessness of their task. Yet the pickers went on picking.

The sun had long passed its zenith, and the shadows were lengthening when, without any warning, I turned a corner of the road to see a notice "Leaving NEGLECTED COUNTY – Entering HOME COUNTY." The contrast was so startling that I scarcely had time to take in the notice. I had to slow down, for all at once the traffic was heavy. People by the thousands swarmed the road and crowded the sidewalks.

I parked the car at the roadside and mingled with the crowd. Smart gowns, neat shoes, showy hats, expensive suits and starched shirts made me a little conscious of my work clothes. Everyone seemed so fresh, and poised, and gay.

I ... made my way further into the trees. Most of the people were carrying a book. Bound beautifully in leather, and edged and lettered in gold, I was able to discern on the edge of one of them the words, "Orange Picker's Manual."

By and by I noticed around one of the orange trees seats had been arranged, rising upward in tiers from the ground. The seats were almost full – but, as I approached the group, a smiling well-dressed gentleman shook my hand and conducted me to a seat.

There, around the foot of the orange tree, I could see a number of people. One of them was addressing all the people on the seats and, just as I got to my seat, everyone rose to his feet and began to sing. The man next to me shared with me his song book. It was called "Songs of the Orange Groves."

They sang for some time, and the song leader waved his arms with a strange and frenzied abandon, exhorting the people in the intervals between the songs to sing more loudly.

I grew steadily more puzzled.

After a while a rather fat man took over from the song leader and, after reading two sentences from his well-thumbed copy of the Orange Picker's Manual, began to make a speech. I wasn't clear whether he was addressing the people or the oranges.

"Which trees do we pick from?" I asked the man beside me.

"We don't pick oranges," the man explained. "We haven't been called. That's the Orange Picker's job. We're here to support him. Besides we haven't been to college. You need to know how an orange thinks before you can pick it successfully – orange psychology, you know. Most of these folks here," he went on, pointing to the congregation, "have never been to Manual School."

"Manual School," I whispered. "What's that?"

"It's where they go to study the Orange Picker's Manual," my informant went on. "It's very hard to understand. You need years of study before it makes sense."

The fat man at the front was still making his speech. His face was red, and he appeared to be indignant about something. So far as I could see there was rivalry with some of the other "orange-picking" groups. But a moment later a glow came on his face.

"But we are not forsaken," he said. "We have much to be thankful for. Last week we saw THREE ORANGES BROUGHT INTO OUR BASKETS, and we are now completely debt-free from the money we owed on the cushion covers that grace the seats you now sit on."

The fat man was reaching a climax in his speech. The atmosphere seemed tense. Then with a very dramatic gesture he reached two of the oranges, plucked them from the branch, and placed them in the basket at his feet. The applause was deafening.

"Do we start on the picking now?" I asked my informant.

"What in the world do you think we're doing?" he hissed. "What do you suppose this tremendous effort has been made for? There's more orange-picking talent in this group than in the rest of Home County. Thousands of dollars have been spent on the tree you're looking at."

I apologized quickly. "I wasn't being critical," I said. "And I'm sure the fat man must be a very good orange-picker – but surely the rest of us could try. After all, there are so many oranges that need picking. We've all got a pair of hands, and we could read the Manual."

"When you've been in the business as long as I have, you'll realize that it's not as simple as that," he replied. "There isn't time, for one thing. We have our work to do, our families to care for, and our homes to look after. We..."

But I wasn't listening. Light was beginning to break on me. Whatever these people were, they were not orange pickers. Orange picking was just a form of entertainment for their weekends.

...Everywhere the ground was littered with fallen fruit. And as I watched it seemed that before my eyes the trees began to rain oranges. Many of them lay rotting on the ground.

I felt there was something so strange about it all, and my bewilderment grew as I thought of all the people in Home County.

Then, booming through the trees came a voice which said, "The harvest truly is plenteous, but the labourers are few: Pray ye therefore the Lord of the harvest that he will send forth labourers..."

And I awakened – for it was only a dream.'[3]

Souls are rotting away. It is not a dream. We have been given care of a world diseased in sin. Each passing day, millions go to the kingdom of darkness forever. Now is the time and today is the day for all in His kingdom to go to war and win souls. This is why we have become new creatures in Christ.

The apostle Paul felt a personal accountability and sense of stewardship for the gospel and gifts committed to him:

- *'...I became a minister according to the stewardship from God which was given to me for you, to fulfill the word of God.'*
  (Colossians 1:25)

- *'But as we have been approved by God to be entrusted with the gospel...'* (1 Thessalonians 2:4)

- *'For if I preach the gospel, I have nothing to boast of, for necessity is laid upon me; yes, woe is me, if I do not preach the gospel.'* (1 Corinthians 9:16)

- *'...according to the glorious gospel of the blessed God which was committed to my trust.'* (1 Timothy 1:11)

- *'[God] has in due time manifested His word through preaching, which was committed to me according to the commandment of God our Savior...'* (Titus 1:3)

- This commandment, which Paul speaks of, is the Great Commission:

  'Go therefore and make disciples of all the nations, baptizing them in the name of the Father and of the Son and of the Holy Spirit, teaching them to observe all things that I have commanded you; and, lo, I am with you always, even to the end of the age. Amen'
  (Matthew 28:19–20)

and

  'Go into all the world, and preach the gospel to every creature. He who believes and is baptized will be saved; but he who does not believe will be condemned.'
  (Mark 16:15–16)

Paul is not alone in this stewardship of the gospel. In 2 Corinthians 5:17–6:2 we are given a clear account of the salvation we have in Christ and our responsibility for the privilege we have received. Paul declares first that:

'Therefore, if anyone is in Christ, he is a new creature: old things are passed away; behold, all things are become new.'
(2 Corinthians 5:17)

Then, in verse 18, he explains how we became this new creature and how we are becoming new:

'Now all things are of God, who has reconciled us to Himself through Jesus Christ, and has given us the ministry of reconciliation.'

As new creatures reconciled to God, we have been given the ministry of reconciliation. As good stewards who have been reconciled to God, we must now minister reconciliation to others.

There is only one ministry in the Church: the ministry of reconciliation – bringing men and women who are separated from God through sin back into a relationship with Him. If a ministry does not have as its ultimate end the reconciliation of the lost, it is not a biblical ministry. This is the ministry God has given the Church. We are stewards of the reconciling blood of Jesus Christ. Jesus, before sending out His disciples, said, *'Freely you have received, freely give'* (Matthew 10:8).

Paul goes on to explain the reconciling work of Christ,

'that is, that God was in Christ, reconciling the world to Himself, not imputing [or holding] *their trespasses to them* [or against them], *and has committed* [or entrusted] *to us the word* [even this word] *of reconciliation.'*
(2 Corinthians 5:19)

In plain terms, we are entrusted with the good news that God forgives men and women's sins through Jesus Christ. The next verse tells us,

'...we are ambassadors for Christ, as though God were pleading through us...'

An ambassador is a representative of a country or kingdom and is responsible for protecting and advancing its interests against or among other countries or kingdoms. Having been invested with kingdom riches, we are now accountable as ambassadors to promote the interests of the kingdom, which is to bring home a bride for the Prince of Peace.

Lastly, in 2 Corinthians 5:21, Paul sets out what Christ did for us: being without sin He took on our sin and made us who are unrighteous righteous (right before God). Reading on to 2 Corinthians 6, we find a verse which is often used as an invitation to the unbeliever to decide now for Christ but which actually refers to those who have received the right-eousness of Christ:

> *'We then, as workers together with Him* [Jesus Christ] *also plead with you not to receive the grace* [God's power and ability] *of God in vain. For He says: "In an acceptable time I have heard you, and in the day of salvation I have helped you." Behold, now is the acceptable time, now is the day of salvation.'*   (2 Corinthians 6:1–2)

Paul is challenging the Church not to waste the righteous-ness received, but to declare the kingdom of God now while men and women have time to be saved. All of our time is kingdom time.

Once, when I was preparing a message on the first beati-tude, *'Blessed are the poor in spirit, for theirs is the kingdom of heaven'* (Matthew 5:3), I discovered that the word 'poor' literally means to have no source of income – to be a beggar. My mind pictured the panhandlers and homeless on the streets of America and those even worse off on the city streets of Nigeria, who have only patches of old clothes or none at all. I reflected that this is what I am like before God apart from Jesus Christ. Without Christ my righteousness is like a filthy beggar's rags. Yet, all who have yielded to Christ's mercy are the greatest rags-to-riches story ever told. God gives to beggars His royal robe of righteousness. We go from beggars to princes and princesses in the Kingdom of God.

He who was rich become poor so that through His poverty we might be rich (2 Corinthians 8:9). I like the World Missionary Press tract entitled 'Who Am I that a King Would Die for Me?' A King dying for beggars? Unthinkable. A King

giving beggars the authority to rule in His kingdom? Not
possible. But it happened, and you and I are the proof.

Our witness to the world is a stewardship of the riches the
King graciously bestowed upon us through His death. Our
proclamation of the gospel is our means of expressing
appreciation for the King who died for us.

Study questions

1. Give two reasons why Jesus Christ is the rightful owner of
   your life.

2. What kingdom riches do you personally possess for
   which Christ will hold you accountable?

3. While on earth, what are we to be stewards of and
   manage?

4. Give an example of the most effective way to exercise
   good stewardship. In the light of your example, would
   you be considered a good manager?

5. How did 'The Parable of the Orange Tree' speak to you?

6. In 2 Corinthians 5:17–6:2 the Apostle Paul speaks of the
   salvation we have received and our obligation to share it.
   Briefly tell how God saved you and how you have been a
   steward of the gospel by witnessing for Christ.

7. Paul stated several times he felt obligated as a steward to
   preach the gospel. Which of the verses quoted would
   best describe you?

Notes

1. New Wine Ministries, 1994.

2. Philip M. Steyn, *In Step with the God of the Nations* (Houston: Touch
   Publications, 1992), p. 231.

3. John White, 'The Parable of the Orange Tree', the author's personal
   collection.

Chapter 4

The Relationship: Covenant Partner – Friend to Friend

*'So Abraham said to the oldest servant of his house, who ruled over all that he had, "**Please put your hand under my thigh, and I will make you swear by the LORD, the God of heaven and the God of earth...**" So the servant put his hand under the thigh of Abraham his master, and swore to him concerning this matter.'*
(Genesis 24:2–3, 9)

When Abraham and Eliezer made this agreement, or covenant, together, they entered into a covenant partner relationship. Keil and Delitzch's Old Testament Commentary says, 'Abraham made the servant take an oath in order that his wishes might be inviolably fulfilled, even if he himself should die in the interim.'[1] Whatever happened, this covenant was to be fulfilled. By requiring him to make a covenant with an oath Abraham was putting his servant under an obligation; he was saying: 'Servant, I want you to swear that if I die before you get a bride for Isaac, you will finish the job. If I never see you again, Servant, I want you to swear that you will bring home a bride for my son' (Genesis 24:2–9 paraphrased).

The swearing of an agreement by placing a hand underneath the thigh of the other party is found again in Genesis 47:29. In this passage Jacob asks Joseph to swear that his bones would not be left in Egypt, but would be taken with them to the land God had promised. This is significant because it represents the idea of posterity. The covenant is for all descendants of all generations. By making his covenant with Abraham, Eliezer was committing not only himself but his children and his children's children to its fulfillment. He is saying: 'If I die, my descendants will bring home a bride. I am making a covenant today by putting my hand under your thigh, that even if I die and cannot fulfill the covenant, my children's children will fulfill it' (Genesis 24:2–9 para-phrased). It was a commitment to preserve Abraham's line.

We are covenant partners with God. When we entered into a blood covenant through the Lord Jesus Christ, we became obligated to carry out our Lord's last wish. Before He left this earth, Jesus' last words, better known as the Great Commission, were,

> 'Go therefore and make disciples of all the nations, baptizing them in the name of the Father and of the Son and of the Holy Spirit, teaching them to observe all things that I have commanded you; and lo, I am with you always, even to the end of the age.'   (Matthew 28:19–20)

Like Abraham, Jesus is saying, 'If I never see you again, I want you to commit to me that You are going to bring home a bride.' Under covenant we are saying, 'Yes, Lord, and not only I, but my children's children.'

When Keith Green made his *Memorial Concert* videotape, he had just returned from a tour of Europe, India and elsewhere with a great burden for missions. He said, 'In an army, the soldiers are to carry out the last instructions of the commanding officer. As far as I read it, the last instructions of our Lord, our commanding officer, was "Go ye into all nations."'[2] Are you, as a covenant partner, obeying the last wishes of Jesus Christ?

In Genesis 15 we read, how, having already promised to bless Abraham, God now made a covenant with him. God has reiterated His promise to bless Abraham with descend-ants as numerous as the stars and to give him a land but Abraham asked for confirmation, '*Lord God, how shall I know that I will inherit it?*' (Genesis 15:8). At the Lord's command Abraham took a three-year-old heifer, cut it in half and laid the pieces side by side. Then he walked through the pieces in a figure of eight pattern. As he walked through the pieces, pointing to the pieces and then pointing to God, he vowed, 'God, be it unto me like these if I do not fulfill the covenant.' Vultures tried to land on the dead animals but Abraham drove them away. When the sun went down, Abraham fell into a deep sleep and God spoke to him:

> *'Then He said to Abram: "Know certainly that your descendants will be strangers in a land that is not theirs, and will serve them, and they will afflict them four hundred years. And also the nation whom they serve I will judge; afterward they shall come out with great possessions. Now as for you, you shall go to your fathers in peace; you shall be buried at a good old age.'*   (Genesis 15:13–15)

Then in verse 17 it says,

> *'And it came to pass, when the sun went down and it was dark, that behold there appeared a smoking oven and a burning torch that passed between those pieces. On the same day the LORD made a covenant with Abram . . . '*

The Bible calls the Lord a 'wall of fire', and so it was the Lord who made the covenant. The word *karath* here translated 'made' can also mean 'cut'. The Lord passed through the pieces and cut a covenant with Abraham. God makes a covenant with human beings. Human beings do not make a covenant with God. He reaches down to people. They cannot reach up to Him.

In Hebrews 9:12, we are told that this new covenant was not made *'with the blood of goats and calves'* – as was made in Genesis 15 with Abraham – *'but with His own blood.'* Jesus 'made' or 'cut' a covenant with us. His body was cut and bled for us on the cross. God reached down to men and women in the person of Jesus Christ to make a covenant with us.

> *'For where there is a testament, there must also of necessity be the death of the testator.'*   (Hebrews 9:16)

In other words, for a testament or a will to be good, the person who wrote it has to be dead. By shedding His blood and dying, Jesus made a covenant with us.

> *'Therefore, brethren, having boldness to enter the Holiest by the blood of Jesus, by a new and living way which He consecrated for us through the veil...'*   (Hebrews 10:19)

When Jesus died, the seamless veil of the temple was torn from top to bottom. He made a new and living way into the presence of God. His death brought about a new will, a new covenant, a New Testament.

What is His will? His will is that none should perish but all would come to repentance (2 Peter 3:9). Hebrews 10:16–18 states:

> *'This is the covenant that I will make with them after those days, says the LORD: I will put My laws into their hearts, and in their minds I will write them ... Their sins and their lawless deeds I will remember no more.'*

God, in the person of Jesus Christ, reached down to us and made a covenant with us. He paid a debt that He did not owe, while we owed a debt we could not pay. We could not make that covenant, but we can share that covenant, cut by Christ, with others. That is our obligation. When we confess Jesus as Lord – when we make that oath – we enter into covenant with God. Paul tells us in Romans 1:14, *'I am a debtor.'* In the New American Standard Version it says in Romans 1:14–17:

> *'I am under obligation both to Greeks and to barbarians, both to the wise and to the foolish. Thus, for my part, I am eager to preach the gospel to you also who are in Rome. For I am not ashamed of the gospel for it is the power of God for salvation to everyone who believes, to the Jew first and also to the Greek. For in it the righteousness of God is revealed from faith to faith; as it is written, "But the righteous man shall live by faith."'*

Paul feels he has an obligation. As part of his last words – a testimony of his life – to the church in Ephesus, he says:

> *'Therefore, I testify to you this day that I am innocent of the blood of all men. For I have not shunned to declare to you the whole counsel of God.'*   (Acts 20:26–27)

We should all be able to stand before God and say, 'God, I am innocent of the blood of all people because I have not failed to share the full testament of God.'

The Lord's Supper affirms the blood covenant between God the Redeemer and His redeemed. As we participate in this memorial, we are saying, 'Jesus, You have delivered me. I am in Your new and living way. Jesus, Your will to see souls saved is still the same and I am committed to proclaiming Your death and resurrection until You return.'

Paul, in Romans 10, recalls for the believers in Rome how they came to faith and then turns their attention to their responsibility regarding the blessing of salvation. He asks four questions:

> *'For "whoever calls on the name of the Lord shall be saved." How then shall they call on Him in whom they have not believed? And how shall they believe in Him of whom they have not heard? And how shall they hear without a preacher? And, how shall they preach unless they are sent?'*
> (Romans 10:13–15)

Four good questions! Are you fulfilling the blood covenant by giving to world missions? Faith comes by hearing. How will they hear unless someone preaches? Are you preaching and testifying? Is your home open for ministry? Are you involved in encouraging and training new believers? They are the next generation to be sent.

When I think of the blood covenant, I think of all those people who have suffered and died so that I could have this gospel today. Their blood has preserved the faith giving us the opportunity to hear and be saved. As Tertullian, a church patriarch, said, 'The blood of the martyrs is the seed of the church.'[3] In his book, *Secret Invasion*, Dave Hunt recounts an

incident experienced by two men who were smuggling Bibles
into eastern-bloc Communist countries. They had been
doing this for ten years and had been put in prison many
times. On one particular mission they attempted to smuggle
Bibles and a suitcase of $10,000 into Bulgaria. The money
was going to be used to print more Bibles in the country.
Their point of contact was a Bulgarian pastor who knew five
languages and had the largest church in Bulgaria until the
Communists took over. (With the kind of intellect that could
master five languages this pastor probably could have come
to the USA and had almost any job he wanted.) When the
Communists came into power, the church was shut down
and the pastor had to go underground. He would not recant
his faith and would not co-operate with the reorganised
church that the government was setting up so government
officials made him sweep the streets with a handleless
broom. The persecution was unbearable and eventually his
wife left him. Not finding him at his house the two Bible-
smugglers located him sweeping the streets. They took him
aside so they could give him the goods. After thanking the
courageous smugglers, the pastor asked only one question,
'When do you think He is coming back?' There was no
bitterness against the Communist party, no bitterness
towards his wife, no bitterness towards God. The only thing
he could think of was, 'When is He coming back?' The pastor
left the two men sitting there weeping. They had been
smuggling Bibles for ten years but they had never experienced the presence of God as they did on that day. [4]

The word 'friend' literally means 'covenant partner', and
friendship is another aspect of the covenant-partner relationship. Abraham and Eliezer were friends in covenant. Jesus is
our friend: He has laid down His life for us. As He Himself
said,

> 'Greater love has no one than this, than to lay down one's
> life for his friends.'   (John 15:13)

Our friend Jesus requests us: 'Friend, I do not have a wife.
Will you bring one back for me?' He appeals to us as Abraham

did to Eliezer, as one friend to another. That is a friendship covenant.

In the Old Testament David and Jonathan made a famous covenant of friendship (see 1 Samuel 18). They exchanged oaths, clothing and weapons. Later, they reaffirmed the covenant and extended it: '... *but you shall not cut off your kindness from my house forever...*' (1 Samuel 20:15). This is the kind of relationship we have with Jesus Christ. He has exchanged His clothing with ours – His robes of righteousness for our filthy rags (cf. 2 Corinthians 5:21). And just as David and Jonathan exchanged swords – representing the taking on of each other's enemies – He takes on our enemies and we take on His. The Bible tells us that Jesus came to destroy the works of the devil (1 John 3:8). The devil is Jesus' enemy and he is ours. In Hebrews 10:13 we learn that Jesus is waiting for His enemies to be made His footstool. Whom is He waiting on? He's waiting on us. He is waiting for us to take up the battle against His enemy. Spiritual warfare is not an option. We are called to fight the good fight. We are called to endure hardships as good soldiers. We will overcome by loving Jesus, not our own lives, even to death (Revelation 12:10).

David and Jonathan swore that their covenant would be **forever**. They promised that if anything happened to them they would look after each other's descendants. After Jonathan died in battle and David became king, he asked if there were any of Jonathan's descendants surviving to whom he could show kindness. David was informed that Jonathan had a lame son, Mephibosheth, and he was brought before David who gave him all the land owned by his father, Jonathan, and his grandfather, King Saul. Then the King declared that Mephibosheth '*shall eat bread at my table always*' (2 Samuel 9:10). This is symbolic of the believer's covenant with God. God, like David, promises to take care of us and our descendants. One day we will inherit the earth and eat at heaven's banquet table. As God promises to take care of our children and their children, we covenant to see that God's line continues throughout the earth. We do this by bringing home the bride.

James 2:21 throws further light on the concept of covenant partner or friend.

> *'Was not Abraham, our father, justified by works when he offered his son, Isaac, upon the altar?'*

Abraham was a friend of God because he obeyed Him. Jesus told us:

> *'You are My friends if you do whatever I command you. No longer do I call you servants, for a servant does not know what his master is doing; but I have called you friends, for all things I have heard from My Father I have made known to you.'*   (John 15:14–15)

How do you know if you are a friend of Jesus Christ? Those who do His will (those who fulfill the covenant – the testament) are His friends (cf. Matthew 12:50). Jesus has been a faithful friend to us; now He wants us to be faithful by doing His will. That is the relationship of a covenant partner. He obligates us with His love. He obligates us as a friend.

Study questions

1. What is your understanding of God's covenant with you?

2. When you came to Christ, did your realise that you entered into an agreement or 'covenant' to carry out His final request (the Great Commission). Explain.

3. What did it take for God to make a lasting, unalterable covenant with the human race?

4. Do you have a sense of obligation or indebtedness to share the gospel? To fulfill this obligation, do you have a 'want to' or 'have to' mentality?

5. What did Paul mean when he said he was *'innocent of the blood of all men'* (Acts 20:26)?

6. What sacrifices were made by other believers so you personally would hear and see the gospel? What sacrifices are you willing to make so that others will hear and see the good news?

7. Over the centuries many people have suffered and died to make this salvation covenant available to others. Name some martyrs you know about and recall their hardships.

8. Name some people who have become children of God through your direct or indirect influence. Those you name are your spiritual children. How can you influence them to carry out the covenant agreement to bring home Christ's Bride?

9. The hymn says, 'What a Friend we have in Jesus'. Do you believe sharing Christ with others is an expression of your friendship? (Read John 15:14, 15; Mark 16:15.)

Notes

1. C.F Keil and F. Delitzsch, *Keil-Delitzsch Commentary on the Old Testament* Vol. 1. (Grand Rapids: Wm.B. Eerdmans Publishing Co., 1980), p. 257.

2. Keith Green, *Memorial Concert*, text from videotape (Lindale: Last Days Ministries).

3. Ruth Tucker, *From Jerusalem to Iran Jaya* (Grand Rapids: Zondervan, 1983), p. 27.

4. Dave Hunt, *Secret Invasion* (Eugene: Harvest House Publishing, 0000).

Chapter 5

The Relationship: Father to Son

'Then Abram said, "Look, You have given me no offspring;
indeed one born in my house is my heir!"'
(Genesis 15:3)

Some years ago the American TV show *The Crusaders* covered human interest stories of people who are doing or have done courageous things. One particular program focused on the Williams family. Pat Williams was the General Manager of Orlando Magic, a professional basketball team in Florida. Although he and his wife have four children of their own, Pat's wife wanted to adopt more. They started adopting street kids from different countries – and eventually they adopted twenty children! *The Crusaders* filmed the daily life of this family of twenty-six. In order for this family to function in an orderly way, everyone had to work together. Each individual had jobs to do and were happy doing them. They began this with their first few adopted children and, in order for them to continue to expand their family, each member had to take on responsibilities. They had to serve. You could not help but notice their gladness. It was apparent that their smiles and joy were not put on for the camera, but were genuine. If I was a street kid from Brazil, Korea or somewhere else, I would be happy to be an adopted son or daughter of Pat Williams, for not only is he a rich American, he is a God-fearing man.

The last aspect of the relationship between Abraham and the servant I wish to focus on, is that of father to son. In Genesis 15:1–3 it says:

> *'After these things the word of the* LORD *came to Abram in a*
> *vision, saying, "Do not be afraid, Abram. I am your shield,*
> *your exceedingly great reward." But Abram said, "*LORD *God,*
> *what will You give me, seeing I go childless, and the heir of*
> *my house is Eliezer of Damascus?" Then Abram said, "Look,*
> *You have given me no offspring; indeed one born in my house*
> *is my heir!"'*

Abraham is complaining that since he is childless Eliezer was
likely to be the sole heir to God's promise. Abraham's words
could be paraphrased, 'This servant is like a son to me. Am I
to adopt him so that he might be heir to the promise and all
that I have?' God quickly reaffirms that the promise of a son
is not figurative but is to be fulfilled literally. Then, as we saw
in the last chapter, God and Abraham make a covenant.

The whole idea of Abraham considering adopting Eliezer
tells us something about the relationship the two men had.
Eliezer, though a servant, was like a son to Abraham, so why
not adopt him? Eliezer was not the son of promise but he was
a son, an adopted son. When Abraham asked Eliezer to go
and find a bride for Isaac, so that God's promise could be
fulfilled, he appealed to him as an adopted son. He deserved
nothing more than to be a servant, but Abraham treated him
as an adopted son. Out of gratitude and love for the father,
Eliezer gladly took on the mission.

Eliezer's relationship to Abraham is similar to our relationship with the Father. Jesus illustrated our relationship with
God with His parable of the prodigal son in Luke 15. When
the prodigal son came to his senses, he rehearsed what he
was going to say to his father:

> *'...I am no longer worthy to be called your son. Make me*
> *like one of your hired servants.'*   (Luke 15:19)

That is how we go to God the Father. We go to Him saying,
'Father, I am not worthy to be your son. Only make me a
servant.' Servants we are, but God calls us to be more. He calls
us sons and daughters.

There are many scriptures which affirm that we are sons
and daughters of God, but two examples are:

'For as many as are led by the Spirit of God, these are sons of God. For you did not receive the spirit of bondage again to fear; but you received the Spirit of adoption by whom we cry out, "Abba, Father." The Spirit Himself bears witness with our spirit that we are children of God, and if children, then heirs – heirs of God, and joint heirs with Christ; if indeed we suffer with Him, that we may be also glorified together.'

(Romans 8:14–17)

'But when the fullness of the time had come, God sent forth His Son, born of a woman, born under the law, to redeem those who were under the law, that we might receive the adoption as sons. And because you are sons, God has sent forth the Spirit of His Son into your hearts, crying out, "Abba, Father!" Therefore you are no longer a slave but a son; and if a son, then an heir of God through Christ.'

(Galatians 4:4–7)

Although we are not 'the' Son, we are adopted by the Father through the blood of Jesus. Having been regenerated by the Holy Spirit, we become sons of God, co-heirs with Christ. And now we can cry, 'Abba Father' which means 'Daddy.' These verses reveal the intimacy we have in our relationship with the Father through Jesus.

God the Father appeals to us as adopted sons asking, 'Will you bring home a bride for the Son of Promise?' Matthew 5:9 says,

'Blessed are the peacemakers for they shall be called sons of God.'

Are you a peacemaker? Peacemakers try to bring rebellious men and women who are enemies toward God in their minds and hearts to be reconciled with God. Before there is peace, there will certainly be conflicts. As a peacemaker for the kingdom of God you will inevitably encounter conflict, persecution and even death. A peacemaker regards adding to the kingdom and God's family more important than his or her own life.

As His children we come to know the desires of the Father and Son and, by the power of the Holy Spirit, we then begin

to fulfill those desires. Founder of Harvest Evangelism, Ed
Silvoso, tells that as a young boy in Argentina he was made to
take an afternoon nap. He had some difficulty settling down
in the middle of the afternoon, so his father would take a nap
with him. Fear of death would grip Ed when he saw his
father's eyes closed. Subconsciously, although he was not
aware of it, he was controlled by the fear of losing his parents
who, he knew, had both lost one of their parents in child-
hood. Ed would lean his ear on his father's chest. Hearing his
heartbeat his fears were put to rest. He would even put lyrics
to his father's pumping heart, 'I love you son. I will not die.'
Relating his experience to the Church's need to hear the
heartbeat of God, he encourages us:

> 'Right now I want to invite you to lean your ear on
> God's chest and you will hear two sounds: none ... all.
> None to perish. All to come to repentance. Continue to
> listen until His heartbeat becomes your heartbeat, until
> you see all of your unsaved relatives and friends,
> neighbors and coworkers, in the monitor of your soul.
> As their names and faces come up, listen to God say,
> "None should perish ... all to come to repentance." ' [1]

Jesus is our example. As a Son He sought to fulfill His
Father's desires; He obeyed the voice and desire of the Father
absolutely. That was the evidence that He was the Son. He
said,

> *'Most assuredly, I say to you, the Son can do nothing of
> Himself, but what He sees the Father do: for whatever He
> does, the Son also does in like manner.'*   (John 5:19)

Jesus is saying, 'I do what the Father tells me and I do not do
anything on my own.' This is how we are to walk. Anointed
by the power of the Holy Spirit He went about *'doing good and
healing all that were oppressed of the devil; for God was with Him'*
(Acts 10:38). Romans 8:14 says,

> *'For as many as are led by the Spirit of God, these are sons of
> God.'*

God brings the Holy Spirit into our lives to instruct us in the ways that we should go. Notice that Abraham instructed the servant in the way that he should go. After Laban had agreed to the marriage, Eliezer bowed down and worshipped God with the words:

> '*And I bowed my head and worshipped the* Lord, *and blessed the* Lord *God of my master Abraham, who had led me in the way of truth to take the daughter of my master's brother for his son.*' (Genesis 24:48)

God will show you the way because it is His heart to bring home a bride for His Son. If you are led by God you will always be looking out for opportunities to witness. It may not always be a situation in which you have to speak, but it will be a witness.

It is the work of the Holy Spirit to glorify or testify of the Father and the Son. Jesus said,

> '*He will glorify Me, for He will take of what is Mine and declare it to you.*' (John 16:14)

The Holy Spirit comes to glorify Jesus. Whom is He going to use to glorify the Father and Son? Us!

Jesus evangelised by revealing God the Father to the people. He was angry with the Pharisees and Sadducees who gave the impression that God was an oppressive and a hard taskmaster. They increased the burden on people's lives by emphasising the rules on observing the Sabbath day and ritual washing. Jesus was angry because He knew that these practices neither glorified nor revealed God. Jesus wanted to reveal God as Father. He emphasised that God was the kind of Father who wanted to give good gifts to His children:

> '*If a son asks for bread from any father among you, will he give him a stone? Or if he asks for a fish, will he give him a serpent? Or if he shall ask an egg, will he offer him a scorpion? If you then, being evil, know how to give good gifts to your children, how much more will your heavenly Father give the Holy Spirit to those who ask Him?*'
>
> (Luke 11:11–13)

By His actions – deliberately healing on the Sabbath, for example – Jesus conveyed that the image the Pharisees and Sadducees were portraying, was false.

Robert Stein writes about Jesus' frequent and unique addressing of God as Father:

> 'The rarity of "Father" as a title for God in the Old Testament and the intertestamental literature stands in sharp contrast with the frequent use of this title by Jesus. It is the way he chose to address God, and it was the way he taught his disciples to address God. Secondly, the use of the term by Jesus is unique in that he gave this designation a warmth and tenderness not found elsewhere.'[2]

It is no wonder that crowds were drawn to Jesus. The love-starved Jews, having only known God as cold and aloof, flocked to know God as 'Abba' Father. Our love-deficient society also needs to know God as their Father. A fatherless generation desperately needs to know a Father who cares for, comforts and disciplines those He loves. 'It is a grand privilege and calling for those who know God as their Father to graciously invite unbelievers to meet God as their Father and not their judge.'[3] They need to see a Father who loves His children equally. They need to observe His children coming from every walk of life united by His love to make up a happy family. Punkers, bikers, Rednecks, Europeans, Hispanics, Asians, Africans, young people, old people, sinners and the once religious self-righteous need to come together to love each other and their 'Daddy' who gave them birth.

In our one-parent generation the invitation to know God as a faithful Father is very attractive. The only ones who can reveal God as a Father to a fatherless world are His children. Evangelism is the family business. The boy Jesus said, '...*I must be about My Father's business*' (Luke 2:49). I believe Jesus at the age of twelve was doing more than probing religious minds that day in the temple; I believe that He was evangelising the religious leaders of His day. Even at that early age, He was trying to make known to them God as Father.

Jesus invited one man to follow Him. The man responded, *'Lord, let me first go bury my father.'* Jesus answered, *'Let the dead bury their own dead but you go and preach the kingdom of God'* (Luke 9:59, 60). Jesus was not being insensitive to the son's need to honor his father. He was saying that 'there are certain things which the spiritually dead can do just as well as believers. But there are other things in life only the believer can do. Let the spiritually dead bury the physically dead. But as for you – be indispensable. Let your main thrust be to advance my cause on earth.' [4]

There are certain things that family members should do! Family members are the only qualified people to evangelise. We alone are qualified because we are the only ones who know Him as Father. Evangelist Leighton Ford tells the story of how he lost his daughter and began to search for her in every conceivable place. As time passed, he said, 'I came to an overwhelming sense that my daughter was lost. Nothing seemed important; every other plan I had for the day was discarded. I went up and down searching every street, alley and corner with one intense, urgent desire to find my daughter.' [5] This is what God feels for His lost creation. No one else can feel the overwhelming, intense desire that God feels for His lost children – no one but you, His family member.

We are unworthy to be His sons, only servants. Yet, He graciously and mercifully adopts us as sons and daughters, heirs to His kingdom, co-heirs to His throne. All He asks is, 'Will you go and get a bride for my Son of Promise, Jesus Christ?' You are the only ones who know what it is like to be a family member. You alone can express the Father's desire to a fatherless world. If you are obedient, when you stand before the Lord Jesus Christ, not only will He say, 'Come in, good and faithful servant,' but, 'Welcome, child of the Most High God.'

Study questions

1. If you were one of the street kids adopted by the Williamson family, how do you think you would feel?

2. What parallel exists between the Williamsons and their adopted children, and God and us?

3. We are adopted into God's royal family of believers. God desires to be the Father of every lost soul in our world. Like the Williamsons' adopted children, our responsible actions will help others coming into God's adopted family. Our joyful obedience to the responsibility of evangelism is God's adoption success. We are not worthy to be sons, but God adopts us and makes us heirs of all He has. How does that affect your zeal for the lost?

4. As an adopted son or daughter, you will be a witness for Jesus Christ. It is by the Holy Spirit that we know we are sons and we know God as our Father. Does your witnessing involve telling others about God as your Father? Explain why it is important to witness to others about God as Father.

5. Witnessing is revealing God as Father to a lost world. What can you tell others about God as Father? Share two examples of God being a Father to you.

6. The Pharisees portrayed a false image of God. Jesus sought to counter this image through His teachings and actions. How does your life (in attitude, speech and actions) portray God as a loving, righteous, merciful and holy Father?

7. Why is it that only sons and daughters can evangelise?

Notes

1. Ed Silvoso, *That None Should Perish* (Ventura: Regal Books, 1994), p. 96.

2. Robert H. Stein, *The Method and Message of Jesus' Teaching* (Philadelphia: Westminster Press, 1978), p. 82.

3. Footnote to verse 14 in *Open Bible: New American Standard Version* (Nashville: Thomas Nelson, 1983), p. 1332.

4. William McDonald, *True Discipleship* (Benin City: Maranatha, 1963), pp. 26–7.

Chapter 6

Our Camels Are Loaded:
Loaded to Attract
Part 1 – Fruits

'Then the servant took ten of his master's camels, and
departed, for all his master's goods were in his hand.
And he arose and went to Mesopotamia, to the city of Nahor.'
(Genesis 24:10)

In biblical symbolism the number ten represents completeness, and the ten camels, loaded with all of Abraham's goods,
represent God the Father loading the Church with all we
need to bring home a bride for the Bridegroom, Jesus. Our
main asset is Jesus Himself, given to us in and through the
Holy Spirit.

Jesus knew the disciples needed to be equipped (figuratively, that their camels needed to be loaded) before they
could establish the Church, and He had promised them:

> *'But you shall receive power when the Holy Spirit has come*
> *upon you; and you shall be witnesses to Me...'*   (Acts 1:8)

The job of the Holy Spirit is to equip us so that our lives will
reflect the Master Jesus (John 15:26). God has equipped us
with the Equipper. The Holy Spirit equips us in two areas: in
the fruits of the Spirit or Christ-like character, and in the gifts
of the Holy Spirit and Christlike service. We will look in this

chapter at how we can have Christlike character and its
power to attract the lost to our beautiful Savior.

In the Beatitudes, Jesus said, 'Blessed are the poor ...
Blessed are those who mourn ... Blessed are the merciful
and the pure in heart...' (see Matthew 5:3ff.). He did not
say, 'Blessed was...' or 'Blessed will be...' but 'Blessed
are...' Jesus emphasised our 'being' because what we are
affects what we do. The result of Beatitude living is found in
Matthew 5:13–14, *'You are the salt of the earth ... You are the
light of the world.'* He did not say that you will be, or might be,
or were, but that **'you are.'** If you are all these 'Blesseds,' then
the by-product is that you are salt and light. You are salt to
a perishing world that needs to be preserved and light to a
misguided generation in darkness. You are going to have
influence and impact in the world because of your Christlike
character.

I was twenty-two years old when I began to attend First
Christian Church in Clearwater, Florida. What impacted me
most was the love and joy of the people who attended there. I
saw husbands loving their wives and kids who enjoyed going
to church. I knew within my sinful life that they had something that I did not have. They were something that I was
not, and this caused me to gravitate towards them.

My father-in-law once said to me, 'You can bring a horse to
water but you can't make him drink, but you **can** make him
thirsty.' I believe God has loaded us with the Spirit of God, so
that the character of Christ will be lived out through us,
making people thirsty for a life in God. Sheldon Vanauken
has said,

> 'The best argument for Christianity is Christians: their
> joy, their certainty, their completeness. But the strong-
> est argument against Christianity is also Christians –
> when they are sober and joyless. When they are self-
> righteous and smug in complacent consecration, when
> they are narrow and repressive then Christianity dies a
> thousand deaths.' [1]

In his book *Lifestyle Evangelism* Joseph Aldrich makes a
similar point:

'... true witnessing is based on what we the saved do
which the unsaved cannot do. Not upon what we the
saved do not do which the saved do. Our witness is not
effective because we do not drink or smoke or go with
girls that do; our witness is effective because we can
perform miracles. A miracle today is when the world
observes husbands loving their wives, wives supporting
and caring for their husbands and families. Church
members hugging, loving, submitting and sacrificing
one to another. When the world sees this they have
witnessed a miracle because it is something the world
has failed to do. When they have seen the miracle, they
have heard the music of the gospel. The music is the
model life you have by possessing the indwelling Christ.
When they see Jesus in our lives, they will listen and
accept our message.'[2]

The historian Ramsay MacMullen wrote a book called
Christianizing the Roman Empire – A.D. 100–400. He says 'that
while Christianity was being presented to unbelievers in both
word and deed, it was the deed that far exceeded the word in
evangelistic effectiveness.'[3] Who we are is going to affect
what we do. In fact, our doing cannot be done in the right
spirit unless we are the right kind of person. It is not going
to be effectual and powerful unless it stems from our life
in Christ. *Charisma* magazine tells of Pastor Steve Sjogren,
who, along with his 7000-strong Vineyard Fellowship in
Cincinnati, Ohio, are working on a program called 'Conspiracy of Kindness.' His church evangelises through kindness.
For example, his members go into restaurants and ask to
clean the toilets. The owners ask, 'What are you going to
charge?' 'Oh, nothing, we just want to demonstrate a practical love for you.' They do many other acts of kindness and
charity because that is what is in their hearts. The pastor said,
'Many people visit the church after they encounter such acts
of kindness. People do not necessarily remember what they
are told of God's love, but they can't forget what they have
experienced of God's love.'[4]

These acts of kindness flow out of who these Christians are.
The Spirit of God ministers the love and humility of Christ

when His servants scrub a toilet in His name. Matthew 5:16 states,

> *'Let your light so shine before men, that they may see your good works and glorify your Father in heaven.'*

Shining our light is equivalent to doing good deeds. Therefore, the lack of good deeds makes a Christian a dimmed light, like one hidden under a bushel. As James says, without works our faith is dead, it is lifeless (James 2:20). Evangelist Leighton Ford likened some believers to shop dummies. 'Some Christians are like mannequins: they do not drink or smoke, they do not do anything, but neither does the dummy, it doesn't do anything.'[5]

Referring again to Genesis 24, we see that the servant travels to Mesopotamia, stops at the well and prays that the girl who comes to draw water and gives him and his camels a drink (v. 14), will be the right bride for Isaac. It was on the basis of her deeds that the girl, Rebekah, was selected to be Isaac's bride. The bride of Christ will be known by who she is and the deeds she does, not by how much she knows. The bride of Christ will not be known by her doctrine but by who we are and by what we do.

Eliezer gives Rebekah bracelets and earrings (v. 22). These represent the fruits and gifts with which God graces every believer. When you become a part of the bride of Christ, the Holy Spirit bestows upon you gifts and the ability to bear the fruit of a Christlike life. Just how effective these fruits and gifts of the Spirit can be in terms of the impact they have on an unbeliever is illustrated in the next verse:

> *'So the young woman ran and told her mother's household these things. Now Rebekah had a brother whose name was Laban, and Laban ran out to the man by the well. So it came to pass when he saw the nose ring, and the bracelets on his sister's wrists, and when he heard the words of his sister Rebekah ... he said, "Come in, O blessed of the Lord! ... For I have prepared the house, and a place for the camels."'*

(Genesis 24:28–31)

Notice what happens here. Worldly, carnal Laban sees his sister and all the gifts, and is drawn. His eyes pop out of his head when his sister enters with ears that sparkle. Laban saw, heard and then ran to see this man of God.

In the book of Acts, we see that this is exactly how evangelism was done in the early Church. Pagan idol worshippers, worldly philosophers and wretched sinners witnessed the miracles. They saw the lives of the believers, and then they heard the message and were converted. That is how it happened then and how it still happens today! People see, hear and then are converted! Remember, Christianity is what we, as Christians, can do that unbelievers cannot do.

> *'But as many as received him, to them gave he power to become the sons of God . . . '*   (John 1:12 KJV)

Anyone can go to church. One can train a monkey to sit in a church service. But living the Christian life takes the power of God. This is the 'Attraction' method of evangelism.

In a book on missions *From Jerusalem to Iran Jaya*, in which she explains the spread of Christianity throughout the whole Roman Empire, Ruth Tucker entitles the first 400 years of Christianity 'The Irresistible Advance.'[6] I like that! Christ has loaded us with His Spirit so that we might lift up Jesus and bring on this irresistible advance. Jesus is irresistible and if we reflect Him in character, others will be drawn to Him. That is why the cleaning of toilets by the Vineyard Church in Cincinnati is such an irresistible act of love.

I was married in my wife's home church. Traditionally at a wedding, the friends of the groom sit on one side of the church and the friends of the bride on the other. As my side only had about twenty people and her side had a couple of hundred, the ushers began to ask friends and relatives of my wife if they would mind sitting on the groom's side in order to equal things up a bit (and perhaps make me feel better). The bride was attractive; nearly everyone had come to see her. As my wife-to-be started down the aisle, the teary-eyed women said, 'She's a beautiful bride.'

A bride who is dressed in white, who is pure and spotless, is attractive. The Church as the bride of Christ is attractive. The

Holy Spirit uses the method of attraction. The holiness and love of Christ's Church make unbelievers gravitate toward her.

Joseph Aldrich explained why people were attracted to Israel:

> 'In a nutshell, Israel's beauty was the beauty of a redeemed people: living, acting and relating in concert with divine will. Evangelism practices the art of influencing the unsaved with the aesthetic sense of which God has endowed His creatures. They respond to beauty.'[7]

Once when my wife and five children were eating at a Pancho's restaurant, we were approached by an elderly Hispanic woman who said, 'You have such beautiful children.' I quickly replied, 'Thank you,' thinking she was referring to their facial features. She then added, 'They are so obedient.' To me, this was a compliment of compliments, because their physical beauty was a gift from birth. The inward beauty this woman saw was developed as my wife and I (mostly my wife) worked with the grace of the Holy Spirit. Often unbeknown to us, the world is watching our character. If it is attractive the lost will become enamored with the person of Jesus Christ.

It is by God's grace that we reflect Jesus Christ in our character. It is by His grace – His enabling – but, that does not mean an absence of work. We labor for fruit. However, gifts are just that – gifts. You can develop a gift but you cannot do anything to receive it. It is like the difference between a fruit tree and a Christmas tree. A Christmas tree just receives the gifts, whereas the fruit tree has to work in order to produce. If the farmer is to harvest anything, he must labor. He must plant, water and plow. In Christ we must do the same in order to produce fruit. We must plow up the fallow, stony ground of our heart in order to plant the good seed of the Word of God. We must water it with prayer in the Holy Spirit. It will require the painful weeding of sin out of our lives, and hard work through the Spirit. But when the fruit of Christ is produced in us, it will result in a harvest of souls. We need to put off the old man and put on Christ because this makes us more usable to the Master.

In 2 Timothy 2:20–21 we read:

> *'But in a great house there are not only vessels of gold and of silver, but also of wood and of clay, some for honor, and some for dishonor. Therefore, if anyone cleanses himself from the latter, he will be a vessel for honor, sanctified and useful for the Master, prepared for every good work.'*

If you cleanse your life, you will be useful to God and prepared for every good work. He is able to use a cleansed and righteous life. Therefore, we should expect the endowment of the Holy Spirit that equips us to minister the gospel. Knowing we have His support gives us confidence to share the gospel. Jesus is our example. The crowds were in awe of Christ's teaching because He did not teach as the Pharisees did, but as one with authority (Matthew 7:28–29). He taught, not quoting the words of others, but from His own experience. He had walked by the Holy Spirit and lived by the Word of God, so when He spoke, it was with authority, and those who heard were awed by His power.

Those who bear the fruit of Christlikeness should expect to be effective witnesses because we are equipped by the Holy Spirit and granted His authority. We should expect Him to load our camels with character traits such as boldness, faith and courage to preach the gospel. You might say, 'Well, I do not have enough boldness.' Reach back to camel number three and pull out boldness. If I need faith, I can pull it from camel number two.

> *'I can do all things through Christ who strengthens me.'*
> (Philippians 4:13)

God has loaded your camels with everything you need. It is there for the asking. So we are without excuse. We need to go out in faith to bring home a bride for Jesus believing that God will supply everything we need.

Agree with God today. Pray this prayer:

'Lord, thank you for loading down my camels. I have everything I need for life and godliness. By You, Holy Spirit, I am a partaker of Your divine nature so others may see your beauty through me and be saved. Lord, let my light shine daily through good deeds so men will glorify the Father who is in heaven.'

Study questions

1. If you are not having an influence in the lives of others as the salt and light that Jesus spoke of, then there may be a lack of 'Beatitude living'. Examine the Beatitudes in Matthew 5:1–16. Make an honest assessment of whether or not you are living them out. Which ones are more evident than others?

2. Recall the character traits you saw in others that made you desire a life in Christ.

3. What is the difference between the fruit and gifts of the Spirit?

4. Do you agree that one of God's main means of evangelism is the attraction method? Why or why not?

Notes

1. Sheldon Vanauken, *A Severe Mercy* (New York: Harper and Row, 1977), p. 85.

2. Joseph C. Aldrich, *Lifestyle Evangelism*. 3rd edn (Portland: Multnomah, 1982), pp. 19–20.

3. C. Peter Wagner, *The Third Wave of the Holy Spirit* (Ann Arbor: Servant Books, 1988), p. 79.

4. Joe Maxwell, 'A Conspiracy of Kindness,' *Charisma*, Vol. 19.5 (December 1993).

5. Leighton Ford, *Good News is for Sharing* (Elgin: David C. Cook, 1977), p. 106.

6. Ruth Tucker, *From Jerusalem to Iran Jaya* (Grand Rapids: Zondervan, 1983), p. 21.

7. Aldrich, *Lifestyle Evangelism*, p. 29.

Chapter 7

Our Camels Are Loaded:
Loaded to Attract
Part 2 – Gifts

'So the young woman ran and told her mother's household these things. Now Rebekah had a brother whose name was Laban, and Laban ran out to the man by the well. **So it came to pass when he saw the nose ring, and the bracelets on his sister's wrists, and when he heard the words of his sister Rebekah,** *saying, "Thus the man spoke to me," that he went to the man. And there he stood by the camels at the well.'*
(Genesis 24:28–30)

When God sends us to do a job, He equips us to do it. He has called us to 'go and make disciples of all nations' (Matthew 28:19). He gave the disciples this assignment and blessed them with the Holy Spirit's power to achieve it. God is the same yesterday, today and forever. He is not going to tell us to do the same job He gave the first-century disciples without equipping us. We have the same mandate as the disciples and we have the same Equipper (the Holy Spirit). The Father has loaded down our camels! He has given us everything we need to bring home a bride for the Lord Jesus Christ.

As we noted in the last chapter, when Laban saw the gifts that the servant had given to his sister, he became very open. When, in the days of the Acts of the Apostles, unbelievers first saw the miraculous gifts of the Holy Spirit, then they believed. Jesus Himself said,

> *'But if I cast out demons with the finger of God, surely the*
> *kingdom of God has come upon you.'*   (Luke 11:20)

Jesus' power proved that He is the King of the Kingdom. When we are operating in the spiritual gifts, we are showing people that the kingdom of God has come upon them. We are demonstrating that they are in the King's presence and not only is Jesus alive, but He is on His throne.

In his book *Power Evangelism*, John Wimber noted how the gifts of the Holy Spirit accelerate the faith of unbelievers as they witness them.

> 'Power evangelism cuts through much resistance (arguments) that comes from ignorance or negative attitudes ... towards Christianity. By penetrating the inner heart and consciousness, God overcomes resistance with the supernatural, resistance that through rational means would take a lifetime – if not more – to overcome.' [1]

My religious background doctrinally did not allow for instantaneous supernatural healings to take place. However, as a missionary in Nigeria, I encountered healings coming from many sources. They were supernatural but not divine. The Nigerians would put their faith in whatever healed them. These people did not have Medicaid or health care insurance. Often it was be healed or die. On one occasion, after successfully preaching at the Okpara Inland Village Crusade, I was counseling about thirty young men who had confessed Christ as Lord or were interested in becoming Christians. I asked them if I could pray for them. One young man asked, 'Will you pray for my friend?'

'Well, certainly,' I replied. 'Where is he?' The small crowd parted and at the back, being held up by two others, was a young lame man. The friend had put him on his bicycle and biked him to the crusade grounds to receive prayer because they had heard that a man of God from the US had come.

'You can't walk?' I asked hesitantly.

'He can't walk and he can't hear out of his left ear,' said the friend.

I thought, 'Oh, God, if you ever did a miracle do one now,' as the faith of some thirty boys was in the balance. What could I do or say? 'I'm sorry but God doesn't do healings any more'? My doctrine doesn't allow for that. The God of compassion wanted me to pray for this young man. First I prayed for his ear. I smothered the good ear with my hand and asked him, 'Can you hear?' He said, 'Yes.' I don't know if his faith increased, but mine sure did. Then I knelt down to pray for his dangling legs. I looked up and asked, 'If God heals you, will you take the message of salvation in Jesus Christ wherever you go?' Again he heard and said, 'Yes.'

'God, this young man needs your healing touch,' I petitioned. 'He has promised he would take your gospel wherever he goes with these healed legs. Lord, I ask that you heal him now so all these men might believe.'

I did not cast or blast out demons. I did not name it or claim it. I prayed holding his legs and I could feel movement as if his ligaments and bones came together. Excitedly I stood and asked, 'Did God heal you?'

'Yes!' he exclaimed.

'Then walk.' He awkwardly took strides to the crusade platform and back.

Immediately, I was rushed by several hundred people. Barren women and men with cataracts were reaching up asking me to touch them. I understood how Jesus felt as the multitudes sandwiched Him. I did not leave for several hours as I prayed for those afflicted with sickness and disease. The outreach was extended for another night and many put their faith in Jesus.

I do not move in the gift of healing as a rule, but God used my prayer of faith that night and on other occasions since then. The point is that the gift brought people to believe the message of Jesus Christ. The Holy Spirit's power is attractive. He attracts the lost to the Lord Jesus Christ when His gifts are utilised.

Often the church operates in the natural rather than the supernatural. Billy Graham said that most of our churches are like Samson. If the Spirit of God were removed, no one would notice. Things would keep on going – business as usual. But the church is a supernatural organism put together by a supernatural God. Leonard Ravenhill once said, 'The church that doesn't operate in the supernatural is superficial.'

As the church, we are to be the beautiful, powerful and efficiently functioning body of Christ. Such a church is attractive. Often, sadly, the church functions like the animal school in this 'Parable of the Animal School':

> 'The curriculum consisted of running, climbing, flying and swimming. All the animals took all the subjects.
>
> The duck was good in swimming and fair in flying. But he was terrible in running, so he was made to drop his swimming class and stay after school in order to practice his running. He kept this up until he was only average in swimming. But average was acceptable. The others (including the teacher) were no longer threatened by the duck's swimming ability. So everyone felt more comfortable – except the duck.
>
> The eagle was considered a problem student. For instance, in climbing class he beat all others to the top of the tree, but used his own method of getting there. He had to be severely disciplined. Finally, because of noncooperation in swimming, he was expelled for insubordination.
>
> The rabbit started at the top of his class in running but was obviously inadequate in other areas. Because of so much make-up work in swimming, he had a nervous breakdown and had to drop out of school.
>
> Of course, the turtle was a failure in most every course offered. His shell was considered to be the leading cause of his failures so it was removed. That did help his running a bit, but he became the first casualty when stepped on by a horse.
>
> The faculty was quite disappointed. But all in all it was a good school in humility; but there were no real successes. None seemed to measure up to the others. But they did concentrate on their weak points and some progress was made.' [2]

By God's grace we have been given spiritual gifts so that we can be successful in Christian living. God has determined that the success of His church should come through Christians using their specific gifts in unity. Gift projection and the push for uniformity of gifts stifle God's formula for success in the church. God has arranged the parts of the body, every one of them just as He wanted them to be (1 Corinthians 12:7).

The great baseball pitcher, Dizzy Dean, probably never imagined that his baseball career would depend upon his big toe. While pitching in the world series, a batter hit a line drive. The ball ricocheted off Dizzy's big toe and broke it. The toe failed to mend properly and, as a result, he could not balance himself as he pitched, causing him to put extra pressure on his throwing arm and ultimately ending his career. His experience illustrates what Paul said in 1 Corinthians 12:26:

'And if one member suffers, all the members suffer with it.'

The fact that as members of the body we are all dependent on one another enhances the importance of each person in the body of Christ. Our uniqueness as individuals in the body of Christ is magnified because we are needed. A spiritual gift is like having a specific job description. We have a specific job in the body of Christ, and without it the body will suffer.

God has given us gifts so that we can be a people of excellence. We watch professional sports because of the excellence of the players. The best team draws the biggest crowds because people are drawn to excellence.

The Holy Spirit is at work bringing many to faith in Christ. Since God has loaded down our camels as a church, it is imperative that we know our spiritual gifts and how to use them. We need to develop and use them to bring home a bride for the Lord Jesus Christ. But, before we can function in our gifting, we must know what our gift is.

What is a spiritual gift? 'It is a supernatural attribute given by the Holy Spirit to every member of the body of Christ.'[3] This means that a spiritual gift is not a role. We have various roles as Christians. We are servants, but not everyone has the gift of service. We are witnesses, but not everyone is an evangelist. Everyone gives, but not everyone has the gift of giving. Everyone is to have faith, but not everyone has the gift of faith. Our gift is not a role or a talent. We all have natural talent and God can use that, but a gift is not the same as a natural ability. It is not a fruit of the Spirit. The fruits of the Spirit create character and the gifts of the Spirit enable us to minister. Therefore we can conclude that a spiritual gift is a supernatural ability that God has given us to minister and bear witness to Jesus. We do this through the body and to the world.

C. Peter Wagner has suggested the following prerequisites to finding your spiritual gift.

1. You have to be a believer.

2. You must believe that spiritual gifts are for today. God will give gift(s) according to your faith.

3. You must be willing to find your spiritual gift(s) and put it (them) to work. You must want it not just to parade around and look good, but because you want to serve the body of Christ. Jesus Christ has given you gifts so that you can be useful. They are enjoyable but their main purpose is so that you can be useful in service to the King.

4. As you pray God will lead you in finding your gift. The Bible says in Luke 11:13, *'If you then, being evil, know how to give good gifts to your children, how much more will your heavenly Father give the Holy Spirit to those who ask Him?'* As He gives you the Holy Spirit, He will reveal to you individually the gift(s) He has bestowed upon you. Not everyone has the same gift. [4]

In Romans 12:6–8 Paul lists some of the gifts of the Spirit:

> *'Having then gifts differing according to the grace that is given to us, let us use them: if prophecy, let us prophesy according in proportion to our faith; or ministry, let us use it in our ministering; he who teaches, in teaching; he who exhorts, in exhortation; he who gives, with liberality; he who leads, with diligence; he who shows mercy, with cheerfulness.'*

I call the motivational gifts of helps, service, and mercy the 'backbone' gifts. People with these gifts are usually found in the background and are often not honored or noticed. But at times these gifts can be more important than other more obvious ones which are often connected with speaking. Paul said, 'They are worthy of more honor' (1 Corinthians 12:23). You cannot see your backbone but could you do anything without one? No! And we know that the people who really keep the body of Christ moving and going are those with the gifts of helps, service, and mercy.

Now consider this attitude encouraged by Paul:

> *'For I say, through the grace of God given to me, to everyone who is among you, not to think of himself more highly than he ought to think...'*   (Romans 12:3)

You need to think highly of yourself – but not because you are somebody but because of who you are in Christ. We must be sure not to think more highly of ourselves than we ought.

Spiritual gifts can also be evangelistic. For instance, you have the gift of service and know that your neighbor and his wife have just had a baby. They have four kids and their grass is growing high. They are frustrated with all the responsibilities of the new baby, and have not got the time or patience to mow the lawn. Perhaps you could mow it for them. If they ask you why you did it, you can tell them that it was a gift of service, and introduce Jesus to them.

Or, if you have the gift of mercy, you could go to the emergency room of your local hospital and minister to those in need of comfort. Perhaps someone you went to high school with might come in and say, 'I didn't know you did this,' and then you could say, 'In and of myself I wouldn't spend my time doing this, but I am saved by the blood of Jesus and God has supernaturally given me a gift of mercy.' The friend might then ask to know more about this gift, giving you the opportunity to share the message of salvation.

As you can see, we need to know what our spiritual gifts are.

'For everyone to whom much is given, from him much will be required.'   (Luke 12:48)

Jesus has loaded down our camels so that we can use those gifts to His glory in order to bring home a bride. God equips us with the spiritual gifts we need to complete the mission to which He has called us.

Here are five ways to find out what gifts the Lord has given to you in order to bring home His bride.

1. **Explore the possibilities.** Study what the Bible has to say about the spiritual gifts. It is very important that you familiarise yourself with them. There are four passages which deal with spiritual gifts, namely 1 Corinthians 12, Romans 12, Ephesians 4, and 1 Peter 4. Find out what gifts there are and how they operate. You might read some books on spiritual gifts. Talk to people who know and have developed their spiritual gifts.

2. **Experiment with as many gifts as you can.** What spiritual gifts have you tried? Assuming you have a right evaluation of yourself, by faith begin to find areas in which you can serve. Are there needs in your local body? Is the need in your area of gifting? If there is a need in the body, then there must be some gifting within the body to meet it.

    Give each gift a fair try. For example, maybe you are teaching adults but you are struggling. You may not have the gift of teaching, or you may just need to try another age group. You might teach children very well. Do not be discouraged if you spend six months or more in an area that turns our not to be your spiritual gift. I spent six years being a pastor and I am not a pastor. I pastored people, though it is not my gift. It is recorded that Thomas Edison made 10,000 attempts before he was successful in discovering the light bulb. A newspaper reporter asked him, 'How do you feel about failing 10,000 times?' He said, 'I have not failed 10,000 times, but rather I have found successfully 10,000 ways that it did not work.' Praise God that there are not 10,000 gifts.

3. **Examine your joy level**. Do you have the joy of the Lord when you are using your spiritual gift? If not, then don't do it. Have you ever said that you hate your job? By the time some people reach their fifties they hate their job and want to quit. How wonderful it is when someone finally gets the chance to find something he or she really wants to do. God is not against you enjoying yourself while you are working for Him. He wants you to 'whistle while you work.'

4. **Examine your effectiveness**. A strong gift in the Lord will get results. Ethel Waters was asked by a reporter why Billy Graham was such a success. She responded, 'God don't sponsor no flops.' Remember the 'Parable of the Animal School.' God has given you a gift so that you can be successful in that particular arena. You are going to see results. That is why God has given us gifts. He is a results-oriented God. I am not saying you have to have results like Billy Graham, but you will see some kind of results. Evaluate your effectiveness. People generally let you know if you are being effective.

5. **Expect confirmation from the body**. Other people will recognise your gift. When I was saved, I went around telling everyone about Jesus, and the members of the church said, 'You need to go to Bible college. You need to be a pastor.' I received confirmation not only that the call of God was on my life, but that there was a spiritual gift at work. You need to pray and ask God, 'How do I fit into the body?' As you start to use your spiritual gift, look for results because you know God's gift will get results. You will be happy in God's employment.

Every member of the body is important. If you were to ask Dizzy Dean before his accident what part of his body was indispensable and would incapacitate him if he were to lose it, he would probably have said his eyes or arms, but not his big toe. The point is that every gift is important. If one gift is not functioning, then the whole body suffers. When the body functions properly, the church becomes a beautiful and attractive bride. Remember that God's method of evangelism is by attraction. People who are in love with Jesus are attractive just like a bride on her wedding day. When the body is functioning supernaturally, people see excellence. God has loaded us with the excellent gifts of the Holy Spirit and through them people will see and believe.

Study questions

1. Do you believe we have the same mandate as the disciples?

2. As you minister, do you think it is important for the gifts of the Spirit to be in operation?

3. Give two examples from the book of Acts where the gifts of the Holy Spirit were ministered causing people to hear the gospel and be saved.

4. Read the 'Parable of the Animal School.' What lesson does this parable teach us? What does the church need to learn?

5. Name the spiritual gift you believe the Holy Spirit has given you. How did you come to know that this is your spiritual gift? Which, if any, of the five steps suggested by C. Peter Wagner did you pass through?

6. Think about the story of Dizzy Dean. Can you remember a time when the local body of Christ suffered when they lost a fairly unnoticeable member because of death, relocation, etc.?

7. Conversely, can you remember how the body was strengthened when certain gifts were added to the church?

8. Access the needs of your group or church. What gifts are needed to meet those needs?

9. If you do not know your gift, it is possible that your gifting may be the very one to meet the needs you identified in response to Question 8. Ask those who know you best to identify any giftings they have seen.

10. How has your gift been used to bring home a bride for our Lord Jesus?

Notes

1. John Wimber, *Power Evangelism* (San Francisco: Harper and Row, 1986), p. 57.

2. G.H. Reaves, *Parable of the Animal School*, the author's personal collection.

3. Peter C. Wagner, *Your Spiritual Gifts Can Help Your Church Grow* (Ventura: Regal, 1979), pp. 111–135.

Chapter 8

Loaded to Unload

'Then the servant ... departed, for all his master's goods were in his hand. And he arose, and went to Mesopotamia, to the city of Nahor.'
(Genesis 24:10)

The Lord has loaded down our camels in spiritual and material resources. Here in the United States we have teaching tapes, books, seminars, Christian TV and radio. We have one church for every one hundred people. It is a near impossibility for an individual not to hear the gospel. People drive past church buildings on every corner, walk past the Christian bookstore in the malls and shopping centers, and catch snippets of Christian broadcasts on the radio or TV. A person would have to work at not knowing or hearing about Jesus Christ. The amount of resources in our country is overwhelming. The Lord has loaded down our camels, and He will hold us accountable. No age in history has had the resources and material ability to deploy the revelation of God worldwide as this era does. We have every spiritual and material resource we need to bring home a bride for the Lord Jesus Christ.

The modern-day prophet Rick Joyner calls this day and age the Laodicean Church Age. The Laodicean church was rich in spiritual gifts and financial blessings and in need of nothing. However, these abundant resources became a curse rather than a blessing. They became dependent on those riches and giftings rather than on the Lord Himself. They became too self-confident. Jesus Christ sternly rebuked them and called them to repentance. However, despite the Lord's devastating verdict on her spiritual condition, the Laodicean church was given the greatest promises of any of the churches named in the seven letters, if she would overcome.[1] The final outcome of this last-day Laodicean church is yet to be decided. Will it overcome?

Because of his one act of disobedience Moses was not permitted to enter into the Promised Land. His punishment by God was, however, just because, having encountered God face to face, he had received a greater revelation than his followers and therefore was held to higher account. According to James, teachers will be judged more strictly than those they teach because they have received greater revelation (James 3:1).

In a term which parallels the Laodicean church concept Rick Joyner also calls our age the Benjamin Church Age. Joseph gave Benjamin, the youngest of Jacob's sons, five times the portion of any of his other brothers when they ate together in the land of Egypt (Genesis 43:34), and this represents the great outpouring of both spiritual and material resources on the Benjamin Church Age. Rick Joyner says:

> 'The abundance of spiritual food in this day exceeds all that of the other church ages and we must take advantage of this great opportunity. The knowledge, understanding, and outpouring of direct revelation from the Lord is given to us for a reason. We are going to need every bit of it to accomplish the mandate given to us in this hour. It is time to buy from Him the gold that has been refined by fire, those treasures of wisdom and knowledge that have been proven. It is time to buy from Him the garments of purity that will cover our sin and nakedness. It is time to buy from Him the eyesalve to open our eyes so that we can see from His perspective.
>
> In Revelation 7:9, we see the great company clothed in white robes who stand before the throne. To the overcomers of the Laodicean church He promises that they will sit with Him on His throne. He has made available to this church a position of authority and

power that is unprecedented. This is not because of our righteousness but because of His purpose for these times. The authority He is about to give has never been needed before as it is now. Those who overcome the spirit of lukewarmness will soon do exploits unequaled in Old or New Testament times. The Lord has saved His best wine for last, and those who are zealous for Him are already beginning to partake of it. The glory of the latter house will be greater than that of the former (Haggai 2:9). This does not mean that the latter (last day) house is greater, but the glory in it will be greater.

We see this promise to the Laodicean overcomer also reflected in the life of Benjamin. When Benjamin was born, his mother died. Before she expired, she named him Benoni, which means "son of my sorrows." Jacob changed his name to Benjamin, which means "son of my right hand." He was transformed or "raised" from a son of sorrows by his mother to the son of his father's right hand. The right hand represents the position of authority and power as Jesus is seated at the right hand of the Father. That the last son was to be named Benjamin was a testimony of the authority with which the last day ministry would come forth.'[2]

Will we be a Benoni or a Benjamin to Jesus? Will we cause Him great sorrow or great joy? Will we sit down with Him on His throne or be shamed and our true nakedness exposed on the day of reckoning? Trusting in riches has caused our spiritual slumber. We must be zealous in our relationship toward God and put off everything that would seek to hinder or sever that relationship.

Jesus said, *'You cannot serve God and mammon'* (Matthew 6:24). He did not say, 'It is hard to serve God and money,' or 'It is tricky to serve God and money,' or 'It is exhausting to serve God and money.' He said, *'You **cannot** serve God and mammon.'*[3]

I once heard an internationally known speaker, who was trying to justify the prosperity doctrine, say: 'If it's a sin to be rich, then Abraham was the world's biggest sinner.' This brother had overlooked Genesis 24:10. All Abraham's goods

were on those ten camels. Why? To bring home a bride. We
are blessed to be a blessing (Genesis 12:3). We prosper in
order to proclaim His goodness. Our camels are loaded so
that we can unload. Notice that when the servant was loaded
down he 'departed.' The resources are to be used to win
Christ's beloved bride.

John Calvin wrote about King David:

> '... [W]ho rose above all that men can receive from
> common sense. He could have easily felt that God was
> causing him to prosper, by putting forth his power to
> maintain him over the kingdom. But to know the
> intention of God and to what end he was doing it takes
> far more prudence. Well, it says because of his people
> Israel. So David knew the reason why he was reigning
> (or prospering). It was not for his personal profit, but
> for the common salvation of all. It is not enough to
> recognize the blessings of God, but we must always use
> them properly...'[4]

We are not to have riches to build our own kingdom. We
have been blessed in order to bless the nations with salvation
and to bring home God's beloved.

In the history of God's people there has always been a
resource-to-challenge ratio that has stymied God's people.
Ten out of the twelve spies looked at their resources against
the giant Amalekites and gave a bad report, 'The land is good
but it cannot be taken. We are too small' (Numbers 13:17–
33). The disciples told Jesus to send the crowds home as there
were not enough resources to feed them, but He responded,
'You feed them.' 'What with?' they asked. 'We have only two
loaves of bread and five fish.' As they obeyed the Lord and fed
the multitude, the loaves and fishes increased (see Mark
6:35–44). God will supernaturally multiply our resources if
we are committed to feeding the multitudes. Jesus did not
say create the supply. He said, 'Feed them.' God will supply
those who are committed to feeding.

The widow whose husband left her in debt desperately
appealed to Elisha to help her (2 Kings 4:1–7). 'What do you
have?' he asked. She replied, 'A pot of oil.' She was to gather

as many jars as she could and to pour out her oil into them. She did as the prophet said and the oil did not run out until the last jar was filled. She sold her oil and received enough income to pay off the creditors who were seeking to enslave her two sons in the event that she failed. After she had done so, she had money to spare. The widow was desperate to save her two sons. If only we would be equally desperate to save those whom Satan seeks to enslave eternally, God would miraculously supply. He would pour out the oil – the Holy Spirit – and pour out whatever financial resources necessary until every person, whom the Bible calls 'jars of clay' or 'earthen vessels' (2 Corinthians 4:7), is filled.

It is a biblical principle that if we unload whatever God has loaded us with, He will continue to load us up again. What did the servant do with his master's goods? He used what he needed for the trip and then bestowed the other goods on Rebekah and her family. Just as the servant used his goods for acts of kindness to bring home the bride, so first-century Christians used 'acts of kindness and charity' to penetrate the Roman world with the gospel. [5]

At one time, I had a morning paper route to supplement our income. One morning, a truck broadsided me totaling my Olds Delta 88. The insurance company offered me $1500 and let me keep the car. This was a blessing since before the accident the car would not have sold for $500. Soon after, we heard of some missionaries in Haiti who were in need. My wife said, 'Let's give them some of the money,' and in fact we ended up giving it all to them, apart from our tithe. I told a street preacher who was in need of an engine to come and get the one out of the car. He worked on the vehicle, replacing the hood, fender and doing other repairs until, to my surprise, he was able to drive it to Houston.

A Chinese congregation in our community had an old school bus they had been trying to sell for $1500. Through one of our members, they learned of our need for a bus so we could pick up children involved in projects we were running. They gave us the bus but we found that the insurance and maintenance would be too expensive for us to operate it so we gave it to another needy ministry. Several months later, a local church gave us an old white van saying, 'If you can get it to run, it's yours.' After a few minor repairs it was running and still is to this day. Two missionaries from Mexico whom we supported gave us vehicles. One of them had outgrown his short-wheel based van when his eighth child was born and the other gave us his truck because he was going to Spain. I later sold it for $1200 to help us get to Nigeria in 1991. Our initial giving began a cycle of blessings that would otherwise not have happened.

Has God poured out enough financial resources to send individuals to the 2.4 billion lost, to be a demonstration of the gospel? In the stories of the feeding of the five thousand and the widow in Elisha's day God provided abundantly more than they needed. Is God doing that today? Yes. In fact, according to David Barrett, as of 1988 the combined annual personal income of church members around the world – both Catholic and Protestant – amounted to a staggering 8.2 trillion dollars. Yes, God has supplied. The question is, 'How are we using it?' 'Less than 2% was given to operate organized global Christianity. Only 1% is spent on direct ministry outside the Christianized world and 1/10 of 1% is spent on the hard core unevangelized.'[6] As of 1979 in the USA, the value of religious property alone amounted to $130 billion and is probably over $200 billion today. Though buildings can be necessary, the construction of expensive and elaborate churches often lacks wisdom in light of finances needed to send out workers into the immense 2.4 billion harvest. The gross financial output for buildings conveys the message that we are more concerned about comfort and convenience than the destruction of souls for whom Christ died. Financing buildings was not considered necessary to evangelise in the first century: God provided existing structures, as was the case in Ephesus where the Apostle Paul used the school of Tyrannus to evangelise not only the city but also the whole province of Asia (Acts 19:9).

If acquiring a new structure is necessary, then the faith we apply to seeing it built can also be applied to financing local and foreign missionaries. By doing so, the congregation gets the message that the purpose of the building is to equip and finance laborers to be sent out to reap the harvest. Such is the case of Valley View Christian Church in Dallas, Texas, as Doug Lucas explains:

> 'Last year was another pivotal year. Valley view desperately needs a new building. Attendance now runs above 1,200, and they are bulging at the seams. In addition to normal staffing and program expenses last year, they decided to buy a plot of land at the cost of more than 1.2 million dollars. This led to another one of those meetings. Once again, they prayed and discussed long and hard about whether or not they should raise the spending for missions another percentage point.
>
> After much prayer and consideration, outreach was placed above their own needs. They raised missions to 39 percent of their annual budget – meaning that they now give $500,000 to the cause of Christ worldwide. Interestingly enough, at this very same Sunday morning during their Missions Fair, they were also able to make a very important announcement. The entire $1,250,000 had been paid off, and the land now belonged totally to Valley View. To me this is an excellent illustration of the way that God blesses those churches who reach outside themselves.' [7]

I believe that churches like Valley View should be the norm rather than the exception. They would be if we captured God's heart for people. William McDonald's commentary on Luke 16:9 shows the proper attitude towards money and possessions that every Christian needs to have:

> ' "And I say unto you, Make to yourselves friends of the mammon of unrighteousness; that when ye fail, they may receive you into everlasting habitations."
>
> The mammon of unrighteousness is money or other material possessions. We can use these things for winning souls to Christ. People won through our faithful use of money are here called "friends." A day is coming when we will fail (either die or be taken to heaven by Christ at the Rapture). Friends won through

the wise use of our material possessions will then serve as a welcoming committee to receive us into the everlasting dwelling places.

This is the way in which wise stewards plan for the future – not by spending their little lives in a vain quest for security on earth; but in a passionate endeavor to be surrounded in heaven by friends who were won to Christ through their money. Money that was converted into Bibles, Testaments, Scripture portions, tracts, and other Christian literature. Money that was used to support missionaries and other Christian workers. Money that helped to finance Christian radio programs and other worthy Christian activities. In short, money that was used for the spread of the Gospel in any and every way. "The only way we can lay up our treasure in heaven is to put them into something that is going to heaven."

When a Christian sees that his material possessions can be used in the salvation of precious souls, he loses his love for "things." Luxury, wealth and material splendor turn sour in his stomach. He longs to see the mammon of unrighteousness converted by divine alchemy into worshippers of the Lamb forever and ever. He is captivated by the possibility of doing a work in human lives that will bring eternal glory to God and eternal blessing to the people themselves.'[8]

Wayne Meyers, long-time missionary in Mexico, preaches that we are to turn the corruptible into the incorruptible, the perishable into the imperishable. He suggested to the students, faculty and friends of Christ for the Nations Bible College in Dallas, Texas, that they tape a sign that read **perishable** on everything they owned. The possession then is made available to God so He might inform them how He wants them to use it. George Otis Jr also comments on the subject of stewardship:

'Until we begin living our lives as if one hundred percent of everything we have belongs to God, we have not mastered the concept.'[9]

After studying the book, *Rich Christian in an Age of Hunger*,[10] our congregation of thirty members decided to have a garage sale with the slogan, 'To live more simply, that others may simply live.' We took things we did and did not need – furnishings, first and/or second TV sets, and items from our attics or garages. You know – those things you think you will need one day, but never do. In a one-day garage sale, we raised over $1000 for missions. We did this biannually for several years, eventually sending my family to Nigeria with proceeds raised in this way. I wonder how many evangelists, missionaries and other Christian workers could be supported just by believers in the United States emptying their attics, garages and overcrowded rooms.

'The average Christian family income in 1990 was $19,280. The weekly foreign missions giving per church member was a paltry ten cents.'[11] That is not exactly unloading all the blessings with which we have been loaded. A missionary went to pick up a few items a church member in North-west Texas was giving for his work in South America. He drove onto the twelve acres of prime property that fronted the highway, past 80–100 head of grazing cattle, beyond the brother's oil well, around the horse barn housing a dozen horses, ahead to the two mobile homes, then turned right and backed up his vehicle to the five-thousand-square-foot brick home. There, he picked up some old clothing, a few battered toys, a moped with a blown engine, old crayons bound in a rubber band and scrap paper on which to draw. All for world missions! These wrong attitudes prevail, but the core of the problem is in our relationship with God.

As we unload, we are kept in that blessed place of sweet dependence upon God to load us up again. Failing to unload can lead to curses. The prophet Malachi rebuked Israel's priests because they were substituting blemished sacrifices for unblemished ones.

> ' "But cursed be the deceiver,
> Who has in his flock a male,
> And takes a vow,
> But sacrifices to the LORD what is blemished –
> For I am a great King,"

> *Says the* LORD *of hosts,*
> *"And My name is to be feared among the nations.*
> *And now, O priests, this commandment is for you.*
> *If you will not hear,*
> *And if you will not take it to heart,*
> *To give glory to My name,"*
> *Says the* LORD *of Hosts,*
> *"I will send a curse upon you,*
> *And I will curse your blessings.*
> *Yes, I have cursed them already*
> *Because you do not take it to heart."'*   (Malachi 1:14–2:2)

The priests' deception of offering blemished sacrifices rather than good ones spoke of their relationship with God. It was cheap: it did not mean anything to them. We were not redeemed with silver or gold but with the precious blood of our Savior, Jesus Christ. When we offer less than our best we cheapen the cost of the cross.

The priests in Malachi 2:2 were already cursed but they did not realise it. The Laodiceans thought of themselves as most blessed; in fact, they were poor, wretched, blind and naked, but they failed to recognise their condition. The deceitfulness of riches had done its job of choking out the spiritual life from these two groups. The greedy person is an idolater and has no inheritance in the kingdom of Christ (Ephesians 5:5). God intended to bless the priests and Laodiceans in order that they could be a blessing for all peoples. Through disobedience the blessing became a curse.

Remember we are loaded to unload. Our camels are packed by the God who owns the cattle on a thousand hills. As we unload, He will load us up again until every member of His bride is brought safely home. He will load us down with what is needed until every pilgrim of the multitude has tasted of the Bread of Life – until every earthen vessel that can be filled is filled. Then, having made friends of unrighteous mammon, a major welcoming party awaits us in heaven.

Study questions

1. Read Genesis 12:3. Why did God bless Abraham?

2. Do you believe the Church is in the Laodicean era? If it is, our fate is still undecided. We will decide it. Are you and your church a Benoni or a Benjamin? Why?

3. Do one or all of the following this week:
   (a) Count how many Bibles you and your family own.
   (b) Number the Christian media communications to which you have access (e.g. radio, TV, etc.).
   (c) On your daily route, count how many church build-ings do you pass.

4. Reread William MacDonald's commentary on Luke 16:9 on page 87. Reflect whether you have made 'friends' through your faithful use of 'unrighteous mammon.' What can this say about where your heart is?

5. The Lord does not expect us to give any more or any less than our best. Evaluate your giving in light of the resources available to you. How is your relationship with God? How much do you value it? Is it rich with heaven's heart?

6. Read 2 Corinthians 8:1–5 (the poor brethren in Mace-donia). How did they give (v. 5)? Paul gives the reason why they could give in this way. They had abundant life. Explain why.

7. If we give sacrificially out of guilt after having read this chapter, we will be in bondage. We will give begrudg-ingly and think the Lord is a hard taskmaster. We must evaluate our relationship with the Lord Jesus Christ and give ourselves wholly to Him and all else will be academic. Take time to do that. Surrender all. Then listen for instructions.

8. **Activity**: make perishable/imperishable cards and put them on items in your home or house in which you meet. Ask yourself if these perishable items could be used to benefit the kingdom. Could you sincerely give them up so God could use them?

9. **Project**: have every member of your home cell group clean out closets, etc. Sell the items the Lord says you don't need. Give the money to **His** work – missions, street ministry, crisis pregnancy, etc. Have a garage sale for missions with the slogan 'To live more simply so that others may simply live.'

Notes

1. Rick Joyner, *The Harvest* (Springdale: Whitaker House, 1993), p. 82.
2. *Ibid.*, pp. 84–85.
3. George Caywood, *Escaping Materialism* (Sisters: Questar, 1989), p. 60.
4. John Calvin, *Sermons on II Samuel*, tr. Douglas Kelly (Carlisle: The Banner of Truth Trust, 1992), p. 202.
5. Ruth Tucker, *From Jerusalem to Iran Jaya* (Grand Rapids: Zondervan, 1983), p. 26.
6. David B. Barrett and Todd Johnson, *Our Globe and How to Reach It* (Birmingham: New Hope, 1990), p. 27.
7. Doug Lucas, 'A Vision for World Mission – Valley View Style,' *Christian Standard* Vol. 128 (30 May 1993).
8. William McDonald, *True Discipleship* (Benin City: Maranatha, 1963), pp. 32–3.
9. George Otis Jr, *The Last of the Giants* (Tarry Town: Chosen Books, 1991), p. 240.
10. Ronald Sider, *Rich Christians in an Age of Hunger* (Downers Grove: Inter Varsity, 0000).
11. Barrett and Johnson, *Our Globe and How to Reach It*, p. 25.

Chapter 9

Loaded with the Law

*'Then the servant took **ten of his master's camels...**'*
(Genesis 24:10)

'O God, give me something that will make them mad or glad. Lord, at this point, a bad reaction would be better than no reaction at all. I need something that will touch their lives, that will cause them to hear.' This is what I prayed one afternoon on my kitchen floor after preaching in the streets of Bryan, Texas, and getting no response. I had my Bible open at Romans 3, and there I found God's answer, specifically in verse 20: 'No one is justified by the Law.' A light went on in my head. I began preaching, 'If you do not accept Jesus Christ as your Lord and Savior, then you have only one other chance to go to heaven. If you've kept God's standard without fail, you will be able to enter God's heaven. The law by which you will be judged, if you reject Christ, is God's Law – known as the Ten Commandments. As I share them with you, be honest and ask if you've kept each one perfectly from birth until now. Number one says...' This was now my preaching. I got reactions.

I also made up a door-to-door survey based on the Ten Commandments, with the aim of finding out how many Americans believed the Ten Commandments were a code of conduct by which we should live and whether or not they personally adhered to it. At the time, Russia was becoming more open and I heard on CBN, better known as The 700 Club, that the authorities were now putting the Ten Commandments in public places like schools. I opened the survey by saying, 'Communist Russia is a self-proclaimed atheistic country and yet today they are putting the Ten Commandments in public places to say they believe this is a code of conduct by which to live. America is supposedly a God-fearing country. Our money says "In God we trust." Yet, the Ten Commandments are not allowed to be hung up on the walls of our public institutions.' People were asked to respond to ten quick questions, and, if they agreed, I would proceed to read out the commands to them and ask if they had kept each one.

Frankly, I got a good bit of flack from my fellow Christian for using such tactics. 'This is the age of grace and using the Law seems to lack love. Besides you do not see anyone else evangelising that way.' It was true. I did not know anyone else using this approach, and I was getting most discouraged. However, in early 1990, I met Ray Comfort at the Houston Evangelism Conference, and he encouraged me greatly. At that time Ray, who was not as nationally known as he is today, preached daily in the streets of New Zealand primarily using the Law. He had done a great deal of biblical and historical research into its use, and God had also given him revelation and insights which I needed to hear. You can find those gems in his book, *Hell's Best Kept Secret.*[1]

I have already referred to the fact that the number ten – the number of camels taken by Eliezer – represents completeness or fullness. The Ten Commandments are a complete, concise summary of the moral nature of God. We have been given the full revelation of how we are to conduct ourselves and by following these commands we become like God.

The first four commands deal directly with our relationship with God. The remaining six deal directly with our conduct towards our fellow human beings, but indirectly also reveal our relationship with God. As John wrote,

> '...for he who does not love his brother whom he has seen, how can he love God whom he has not seen?'
>
> (1 John 4:20)

This perfect revelation of God discloses the imperfection of our relationship with Him. God has given us the Law to show us how far apart we are from Him. God's intention is that once exposed as sinners, separated from Him, we would call on His Son who can reconcile us to the Father.

God also intends for us to use the Ten Commandments as a means of evangelising the lost. Galatians 3:24 states that *'the law was our tutor to bring us to Christ.'* We learn from 1 Timothy 1:8:

> *'The Law is good, if anyone uses it lawfully – for the purpose for which it was designed.'* (Amplified Bible)

The next verse tells us whom it is for:

> *'... knowing this: that the law is not made for a righteous person, but for the lawless and insubordinate, for the ungodly and for sinners, for the unholy and profane...'*
> (1 Timothy 1:9)

Putting these two passages together we realise that the Law is like a schoolmaster bringing the sinner, the ungodly, unholy individual, to Christ. As believers, our purpose in using the Law is to expose to the unsaved that their sin is *'exceedingly sinful'* (Romans 7:13) and that they need the forgiveness of the Savior.

In the Amplified Bible, Romans 2:15 says,

> *'They show the essential requirements of the Law are written in their hearts and are operating there, with which their conscience (sense of right and wrong) also bears witness...'*

The Law is written into the heart of every one of us. Therefore, when we hear the commandments, we instinctively know they are true. Instinctively we know that the Law reveals the nature or character of God and that, as Genesis 1:28 says, we were originally made in His likeness. Intrinsically, we know these things to be true. The word 'conscience' in Latin means 'with' (*con*) 'knowledge' (*scire* – to know). The sinner knows that these commands are true and that he or she has violated that truth. As Romans 3:20 says, through the

Law we come to the knowledge of sin. Once people come to the knowledge of sin, then they see their need of a Savior.

A.B. Earle, a Baptist preacher who saw 150,000 men and women come to Christ, said, 'I have found by long experience, that the severest threatening of the Law of God have a prominent place in leading men to Christ. They must see themselves lost before they will cry for mercy. They will not escape danger until they see it.'[2] John Wesley agreed that, 'Before I can preach love, mercy and grace, I must preach sin, Law and Judgment,'[3] and C.H. Spurgeon said, 'They must be slain by the Law, before they can be made alive by the gospel.'

Usually, after I have started a casual conversation with someone I have just met, I will ask a few diagnostic questions. These questions are taken from Dr James Kennedy's Evangelism Explosion program and help to identify what the individual is trusting in for his or her salvation. They are:

1. If you died tonight, do you know for certain that you would go to heaven?
2. If you died tonight and had to stand before God, and He were to ask you, 'Why should I let you into heaven?' what would you say?

Most frequently, people will say that being good and obeying the Ten Commandments will get them into heaven. I usually ask them to recite the Ten Commandments. They can sometimes quote a few, but usually not all of them. I then offer to go through them and follow each explanation by asking whether or not he or she has kept that particular commandment.

'You shall have no other gods before Me.'[4] Jesus said it this way:

> *'You shall love the Lord your God with all your heart, with all your soul, with all your mind, and with all your strength.'*
> (Mark 12:30)

Can you say you have always loved God with everything you have? Usually, the god we put before Him is ourselves. We love to do what we want and become a god to ourselves, serving ourselves.

'You shall not make for yourself a carved image.' This means we are not to worship idols –anything that has been created – but only the Creator. To find out if you worship anything other than God, reflect on what you spend your time doing, thinking and talking about. If it is not Jesus Christ, then you probably have another god. If you serve it with your time, thinking and speech, you are worshipping it. You can also make your own image of God from your own imagination. For example, when we make such statements as 'I do not believe a loving God would create hell' we are creating God in our own image, not as He really is, and this is idolatry.

'You shall not take the name of the Lord your God in vain.' This means you must not use His name in a flippant, irreverent or meaningless fashion. If you stub your toe and say 'O God,' you have broken this command. Why do we attribute something bad to God? Why not say, 'O Hitler'? Our mouths reveal our hearts. We do not use our mother's name in this way because we love our mothers. If we loved God, we would not use His name in that manner either.

'Remember the Sabbath day, to keep it holy.' Can you say you have always taken one day out of seven to worship God?

'Honor your father and mother.' Have your father and mother ever disciplined you? Disobedience dishonors them. Every child has been disobedient at some time or another.

'You shall not murder.' 'Oh, I haven't done this one.' But Jesus said:

> *'You have heard that it was said to those of old, "You shall not murder, and whoever murders will be in danger of the judgment." But I say to you that whoever is angry with his brother without a cause shall be in danger of judgment ... But whoever says, "You fool!" shall be in danger of hell fire.'*
> (Matthew 5:21–22)

Have you ever been angry without a good reason? Or called someone a name? The Bible tells us that if we act in this way, we are murderers in our hearts.

'You shall not commit adultery.' This includes pre-marital sex, sex outside marriage and sex with another person's husband or wife. Jesus also said:

> 'You have heard it was said to those of old, "You shall not commit adultery." But I say to you that whoever looks at a woman to lust for her has already committed adultery with her in his heart.'   (Matthew 5:27–28)

Do you ever look at women (or men) lustfully, or even photos wishing the picture would come alive? Have you broken this commandment?

'You shall not steal.' It does not matter how big or small: it could be a pen or paper clip; it could be cheating on your income tax or borrowing something without returning it.

'You shall not bear false witness...' Rumors, fibs, white lies, and exaggerations are included. How many lies does it take to become a liar? Just one.

> 'All liars shall have their part in the lake which burns with fire...'   (Revelation 21:8).

'You shall not covet...' This is the desire for more and more. Most of us have wanted more, sometimes desiring something that belongs to another. The Bible tells us that covetousness is idolatry (Colossians 3:5). If you have coveted, you have also committed idolatry. If you have stolen, you have also been covetous. The apostle James writes:

> 'For whoever shall keep the whole law, and yet stumble in one point, he is guilty of all.'   (James 2:10)

When I witness to individuals by using the Ten Commandments I ask them how many they are aware they have broken. I have never had anyone say they have broken less than five. They and all of us will have to stand before God, not man, having broken at least five commands. God says, 'The guilty will not go unpunished' (Exodus 34:7). Will you be punished?

I tell them that, on that day, they will not succeed in justifying themselves. They will not be able to stand before the Judge and say, 'I think you should let me go because I only broke five and the next guy broke eight.' Or, 'Judge, I'd like you to consider all the people that I didn't lie to, steal from, lust after...' No, we will be judged for what we have done.

Any good deeds we think we may have done do not cancel out the wrong we have done. Jesus said, '...*he who does not believe is condemned already'* (John 3:18). A man on death row condemned to death does not have to commit any more bad deeds in order to die. What he has done constitutes enough to condemn him. In the same way the law has shown that we are already condemned. We have committed enough sin. We do not have to lie, commit more thefts, or have more impure thoughts. We have already done enough to send us to hell.

Then I ask the person to whom I am speaking about whether he or she believes a man called Jesus Christ existed and died a cruel death on the cross. Then I tell them that the Bible says Jesus was without sin. He was totally innocent, yet was unfairly crucified for our sins. Jesus was not the outlaw: we were. He was not the criminal: we were. He literally took our place by dying a criminal's death and paying the penalty for our sins. Every wrong lustful thought, every theft ... whatever it was, regardless of how many times we did it, Jesus paid for it on the cross.

When Jesus was on the cross, He said, 'It is finished.' He was saying, 'Paid In Full.' Jesus paid for our sins in full so we do not have to pay for eternity in hell. Our sins are finished in God's sight. Whatever the crimes committed against God, He loves us and forgives us through His Son, Jesus Christ. When I have explained the gospel fully, I go on to lead anyone who is ready to repent of his or her sins to receive God's forgiveness and to put his or her faith in the death and resurrection of Jesus Christ, and confess Him as Lord.

By just going through the commandments, you begin to sense the other person's feelings of condemnation and hope-lessness. For those lost in sin, this is good because in their day-to-day lives they have too many things giving them a false sense of security that they do not realise their lost state. Once they know they are helpless, hopeless and condemned before God's Law, then we can give them God's mercy and love if they cry out for it. Americans have heard that Jesus loves them so much that they often do not appreciate it. Paul tells us that *'the message of the cross is foolishness to those who are perishing'* (1 Corinthians 1:18). It does not make sense unless we can understand that God mercifully took the punishment we justly deserve.

At first, this approach of facing people with God's Law does not appear loving, but in actual fact it is the most loving way. It brings the sinner to true contrition and salvation. People gain a thorough understanding of what they have been saved from and saved to. They know they have sinned much and therefore have been forgiven much. As a result they will themselves love much – both God and others.

This approach works everywhere. When I used it in an Anglican church in the USA, old ladies and men with religion, but without a relationship with Christ, came running forward and fell on their knees weeping in repentance. Among the unreached Ijaw tribe in Nigeria, thirty men came forward after I had spoken to them about the Law, and most of these men showed the genuine fruit of salvation.

> *'The law of the Lord is perfect converting the soul.'*
> (Psalm 19:7)

Use the perfect weapons, in order to bring home the bride. First, the Law of God, then the love of God. In the words of Ray Comfort, 'with the sickle of God's Law in your hands, you become a laborer, not a layabout, a soul-winner not a pew warmer, an asset not a liability.'[5] We can be loaded down and not know where to go. Being loaded is essential, but being led is equally necessary. Prayer leads the way.

Study questions

1. **Activity**: make up a role-play of a soul-winning situation using the Ten Commandments.

2. What do Romans 3:20 and Galatians 3:24 say the purpose of the Law is?

3. According to 1 Timothy 1:8–9 whom is the Law for?

4. Why do you think the Law is effective? Why will it be effective for every human being?

5. Have you ever used the Ten Commandments in evangelism?

6. Do you believe a sinner will more fully understand and appreciate the love demonstrated to us by the cross of Christ when he or she has first understood the relevance of the Law? Why or why not?

7. Why do most people not use the Law? Do you think it is unloving? When do you think it is inappropriate to use it?

8. Speaking honestly, are you afraid even to attempt to use the Law in evangelism? Why?

9. **Activity**: give one commandment to each person present and ask him/her to explain it briefly. Then have each person record how many commandments they have broken in their life.

10. **Project**: make a list of relations for whom you have been praying that they will be saved. Make an appointment to witness to them using the Law. On a later occasion share the results with the group. Or, ask someone in your group who is more experienced if you can accompany him/her on an occasion when he/she will use this method of evangelism.

Notes

1. Ray Comfort, *Hell's Best Kept Secret* (Springdale: Whitaker, 1989).
2. Quoted in Comfort, *Hell's Best Kept Secret*, p. 25.
3. Quoted in Comfort, *Hell's Best Kept Secret*.
4. The Ten Commandments are found in Exodus 20:1–17.
5. Comfort, *Hell's Best Kept Secret*.

Chapter 10

Camel Caravan or Calamity?

There is only one set of people who can answer the prayer of Jesus in John 17, *'they may be made perfect in one'* (v. 23). Those same people are the only ones who can hinder that prayer from being fulfilled. It is not the Communists, Buddhists, or the Muslims. You know those people. You meet with them regularly. In fact, you are probably one of them. It is the Church! Unity was so important to Jesus that He prayed for it four times in one prayer (John 17:11, 21, 22, 23). This is the only record of Jesus praying four times for any one thing.

From Jesus' prayer in John 17, we can deduce that:

1. unity or oneness is the very nature of God;
2. since it is the will of the Father and the Son, not to strive for it is to be outside His will; and
3. it is His purpose for the Church.

As my friend, Dr Terry Teykl, has said, 'Jesus is coming back for a bride, not a harem.' The outgrowth of biblical unity is so *'that the world may believe that You sent Me'* (John 17:21). It is through unity that Jesus the Son is revealed to our communities and to the world. To hinder unity is to hinder God's revelation on the earth.

How does this relate to Eliezer and the story of Genesis 24? As we mentioned in Chapter 7, 'Our Camels Are Loaded', we have the resources, especially in the United States. God has loaded down all our camels (the Church) with all we need to bring home a bride for Christ. The problem is the camels are named Methodist, Baptist, Assembly of God, Church of God, Presbyterian, etc., and none of them are connected. The reality is that these camels, representing the various church denominations, are loaded down going their separate ways, often using their resources for something other than their God-ordained purpose. There is no sense of a network or caravan where the various parts are working together in a common objective – to win lost souls. We are doing something other than 'God's Soul Desire.' It is not only a denominational problem but occurs at grassroots level with the local churches in our communities and cities.

A good friend of mine, Pastor Leonard Lord, said, 'Satan has no power except that which we give him through division.' Think about that statement. When the enemy is at work in your family, job, church, etc., division can usually be found. Jesus told us the way to defeat an opposing kingdom is to divide it (Mark 3:24).

In response to the call for unity, one large mega-church pastor told me, 'It's all those smaller church pastors who need the unity. They are the ones who get into it.' I felt like saying, 'You mean those little guys like Jack Hayford and Ted Haggard? Both of those men who have churches in excess of 7,000 members but lead the unity efforts in their cities?' It is not a question of micro-church or mega-macro-church. The question is, 'Is this the will of the Father and the Son?' Absolutely! This is the heart of the Father. Therefore, a big church not using its health, vitality and resources to encourage other congregations of the Church in the city as a whole is missing God **in a very big way**. I believe the scripture that says, *'For everyone to whom much is given, from him much will be required'* (Luke 12:48), applies here.

Paul told the church in the city of Philippi:

> *'Only let your conduct be worthy of the gospel of Christ, so that whether I come and see you or am absent, I may hear of your affairs, that you stand fast in one spirit, with one mind striving together for the faith of the gospel.'*
>
> (Philippians 1:27)

For Paul conducting oneself in a manner worthy of the gospel meant being of one mind and one spirit, striving together. Anything less is unworthy conduct. We are guilty as charged.

At times we find the Church not only not striving together but even striving against one another. We go beyond indifference to being antagonistic. It is one thing to be aloof and distant to one another; it is another to use the resources intended by the Lord for reaching others, in fighting one another. The camels are not merely going in different directions, now they are butting heads and kicking one another. All the while we are losing time and resources while the bride is out there waiting to be won. After the fight, the resources have to be used to heal the camels (churches and their members) caught in the fight. Separation, striving against one another, wasting time, energy, people and material resources, can only be a calamity in God's eyes.

A Baptist preacher was having a special night of revival at his church. He surveyed the crowd and noted that it was dominated by those of his denomination. 'Let me see your hands tonight if you're glad to be a Baptist,' he proudly announced. All raised their hands except one lady sitting near the front. The preacher asked, 'If you don't mind me asking you, Madam, what denomination are you from?' 'I'm Methodist,' she replied. Quizzically he asked, 'Why are you Methodist?' 'Well, my daddy was Methodist, and his daddy and my great-granddaddy before him.' 'Well,' said the pastor smugly, 'if your daddy was a moron and his daddy and granddaddy before him as well, what would that make you?' The lady thought for a moment and then quipped, 'I guess that would make me a Baptist.' When pride keeps us from obeying the Head of the Church, Jesus Christ, and His prayer in John 17, we act like morons. Pride that divides us and allows the enemy to have his way in our communities makes us appear like morons. Our selfishness allows us to squander resources that could be used collectively to reach those in our localities and throughout the world for Christ.

After returning from Nigeria in 1997 I had a sense that God was calling me back to my home town of Clearwater in the

Tampa Bay area of Florida. The mark of the enemy in the area was clearly defined. The Scientology international head-quarters is in Clearwater, and Tampa is a major producer of pornography as well as a leading exporter of death music. St Petersburg was the last city in the USA to have a racial riot. Of course, the problems of crime, drugs, teen pregnancy, etc., are no different from most other cities. We were experiencing calamity because there was no caravan. It was my conviction that if there were a united spiritual front in Tampa Bay these problems could not exist to the same degree.

God called me, my wife, and our six children back to the Tampa Bay area to seek to unite the churches to do together what we could not do apart. Our continued hope is to line up the camels and the resources to do the will of the Master in our community. Understand, we had no denominational backing. We had no place to stay. This was my home town but I had been gone for twenty years. Our only asset was God saying, 'Go.'

God had already gone before us. In six months 126 pastors and ministry leaders signed a Covenant of Unity. At the official signing on 10 June 1997 we adopted the prophetic name which Doug Stringer had given to unity in Houston, 'Somebody Cares', becoming one of the first Somebody Cares cities. The local television station aired the signing, and the response was so great that the program was screened four times. Pastors' meetings began to evolve throughout Tampa Bay. Today we have seven different pastors' meetings in different geographical areas. The vision has mushroomed beyond our borders, and other counties in Florida have now adopted the Somebody Cares concept.

We also brought together the compassion or street minis-tries. God gave me the vision of honoring these ministries who care for the disadvantaged week in and week out. We cast the vision before a group of business people to be 'Businesses Who Care,' suggesting that they sponsor tables at a banquet to honor these unsung heroes of our streets. They took up the challenge, and we were able not only to honor them with a banquet but to give each one a gift. From this we provided the community with a compassion ministries resource directory.

The businesses have funded much of what has taken place with Somebody Cares. We challenge them to see their business as their ministry. Just as a pastor is called to the area, they have been called as a business or professional person to be used in the market-place to extend fully God's kingdom. Most respond to the message. They want to do more than go to church and pay their tithe. They also want to be involved in something bigger than themselves and their congregation. They are business people with a vision to see Christ's gospel impact the whole community.

One of the first strategies we implemented was a prayer evangelism campaign called 'The Year of Answered Prayer.' Churches adopted square geographical areas to saturate in prayer called 'prayer squares.' Twenty billboards were put up, inviting prayer requests from those in need and as a result thirty calls a day were received. Churches displayed banners for the whole year; members put up yard signs declaring their house a 'house of prayer'; bumper stickers, approximately 500 prayer boxes in businesses, 250,000 door hangers inviting prayer requests were distributed. This unified effort brought about a God-consciousness in our communities.

Psalm 133 states that where brethren dwell together in unity *'the Lord commanded the blessing – life for evermore'* (v. 3). We received a commanded blessing. The professional baseball team in Tampa asked us to put on a Christian event at their stadium prior to a game. The event 'Raise the Roof' was created. God had provided a big barn for a big harvest. It was something we couldn't do separately, but we could do together. Christian artists ministered in song and professional ball players gave testimonies. I was honored with the privilege of sharing the gospel with over 16,000 people. This event has been staged each year now for several years and we have seen hundreds come to Christ. Each year the business community sponsors 2,000 underprivileged children to attend Raise the Roof. We are able to present Christ to the Tampa Bay residents at large.

God's commanded blessing is for the purpose of bringing life for evermore. Here is a list of other blessings that have come through our united commitment to bring life for evermore to those in Tampa Bay:

- We led the crusade visitation day for the Billy Graham Crusade in October 1998, visiting 100,000 in one day. It was Billy Graham's third largest crusade ever in the USA. We also led the pastors' prayer meetings and the intercessory prayer.

- We kicked off the National Book of Hope campaign, distributing 500,000 gospel booklets of that title and hitting 90 per cent of all residents in greater Tampa Bay.

- We mobilised over 600 teens for prayer and servant evangelism into the public schools for a forty-day period called 'This Means War.' Dr Bill Bright used forty minutes of testimonies which came out of this on his national World Changers radio program.

- We distributed 40,000 New Testaments and reading guides encouraging reading through the New Testament in five minutes a day for 'The Year of Good News.'

- Annually we distribute over 12,000 backpacks filled with school supplies, reaching needy children and giving local churches the opportunity to show God's love in a practical way.

- We organised the Supper Bowl as a sanctioned event of Super Bowl XXV, distributing 120,000 lb of food, three truck-loads of clothes and twenty pallets of Keebler cookies. We had free medical check-ups, children's programs, youth bands, and three sports clinics by professional athletes. One thousand volunteers from 175 churches, businesses and ministries joined together. Approximately 12,000 people attended with 1,210 indicating they had made a decision for Christ.

- Currently, on an ongoing basis, we have partnered with the national ministry Operation Blessing, to bring in 30,000 lb of food weekly to aid the outreach of over 200 ministries. These ministries can now spend more time and energy on people than on raising funds for food.

We have seen some great things take place through our united efforts. God wants to do more. The kingdom work in each one of our communities is bigger than any one of us, but needs every one of us! You would expect with such large events and extensive mobilisation of God's people that the cost would be in the hundreds and thousands of dollars. However, most of this was done through our little donated offices and a few staff. How did it happen? As each does his or her part, it adds up to a greater whole that makes a powerful impact. When the camels (churches) become the caravan, each doing its part and sharing resources, more can be accomplished with less.

God has loaded our camels. As we work together, we maximise our resources so all those whom God longs to make part of His bride can be reached. Our resources go farther and we can do better and bigger things than we could ever imagine. Of course, that is just from the practical side. Add the spiritual equation of God's commanded blessing and the potential impact is unlimited.

Who would be willing to live outside of God's commanded blessing for their communities? No one, I'd imagine. However, many are doing just that. We will discover the commanded blessing of Christ's presence in our communities as we obey Him and dwell together in unity. I believe God still wants to see the Church as the head and not the tail. As children of light, we should be the greatest influence in our communities, not those in darkness. We will be the head and not the tail, as we line up with the Head, Jesus Christ.

Our various congregations, ministries, businesses and individual talents make up what Doug Stringer calls 'a mended net.' We will get far better results together creating a net than our individual poles. A great end-time harvest is taking place. If the mended net in your city is in place, the catch is sure to happen.

We have experienced the calamity of wasted resources. The cities of our nation have suffered because our influence has been dimmed. It is time for the Church to be a caravan of camels loaded down with resources and pursue with all her heart God's soul desire which is to find His bride.

Study questions

1. Do you believe it is God's will for the Church to be one? What other scriptures can you find to substantiate your belief?

2. Identify the work of the enemy in your city.

3. Is part of the calamity due to the fact that the Church is not a caravan?

4. Is there a group of churches and pastors coming together to fulfill John 17? If so, see how you can serve them as they work together to reach your community. Pray for more pastors to join them. If the pastors aren't working together, begin to pray for them to catch the vision and the need to be God's caravan. Invite others to join you in prayer. Begin noting answers to your prayers.

5. Have you stayed away from others who are different from you denominationally or racially? What can you do to change?

6. Make an appointment to speak to your pastor about this issue.

7. Do you think Jesus considered unity among His people to be optional? If not, is any excuse a good excuse, or just disobedience?

8. Have you seen God bless your community or others as a result of churches being obedient and serving their cities together?

9. Take this week to pray, asking God to show you your part of God's caravan of believers. Write down the answer.

Chapter 11

Praying for Appointments

*'Then he said, "O Lᴏʀᴅ God of my master Abraham, **please**
give me success this day, and show kindness to my master
Abraham. Behold, here I stand by the well of water; and the
daughters of the men of the city are coming out to draw water.
Now let it be that the young woman to whom I say, 'Please let
down your pitcher that I may drink,' and she says, 'Drink, and I
will also give your camels a drink' – let her be the one You have
appointed for Your servant Isaac. And by this I will know that
You have shown kindness to my master."'*
(Genesis 24:12–14)

Our Lord is faithful to His covenant. Deuteronomy 7:9 states:

> *'Therefore know that the Lᴏʀᴅ your God, He is God, the
> faithful God who keeps covenant and mercy for a thousand
> generations with those who love Him and keep His
> commandments.'*

Numbers 23:19 also emphasises that God is always true to His
word:

> *' "God is not a man, that He should lie,*
> *Nor a son of man, that He should repent* [change his
>   mind].
> *Has He said, and will He not do?*
> *Or has He spoken, and will He not make it good?"'*

Andrew Murray said, 'If we were but to grasp what God desires to do for us, and if we understood the nature of his promise it would make covenant the very gate to heaven.' [1] We will learn in this chapter that not only has God made a covenant with us to get us to heaven, but that He has also given us covenantal promises in prayer which we can claim in order to bring others to heaven's gates as well.

When God made His covenant with Abraham, He obligated Himself to bless Abraham, to make his name great and make him the father of many nations (Genesis 12:2–3). Abraham had faith that God would do as He promised. The servant knew of this covenant, and he had witnessed Abraham's faith in God. Now, the servant himself had to put his faith in that covenant in order to find a bride for Isaac. When he had questioned his master about the likelihood of success on this mission, Abraham had assured him that Jehovah, the God who keeps His promises, had sent an angel ahead of him and guaranteed the success of the venture (Genesis 24:7).

God has also promised that we will be successful in bringing home a bride for Jesus Christ. He has promised that His bride would be made up *'of every tribe and tongue and people and nation'* (Revelation 5:9). He has promised that His name would be great among the Gentiles (Malachi 1:11) and that we would have the nations as our inheritance (Psalm 2:8). He has promised that cities and whole nations will come to know Jesus Christ as Lord (Zechariah 8:20, 22; Psalm 86:9).

As Christ's kingdom is established on every shore and among every people, God continues to demonstrate His faithfulness to Abraham and to us, for you and me as believers in Christ are the fulfillment of His covenant to Abraham. Yet, today we are observing a growth in Islam of 26,000 members every year, and a resurgence in occultism and witchcraft through the New Age Movement; the cry of liberal America gets louder and a dark cloud of violence and sex covers our streets. These evil obstacles appear too formidable for the Church to penetrate. Yet we must always keep in mind that it is not our power that is the deciding factor.

In 2 Chronicles 20, Jehoshaphat was surrounded by three armies from enemy countries. Overwhelmed, he *'feared and* *set himself to seek the L*ORD*'* (2 Chronicles 20:3). Turning to God, he desperately prayed God's promise,

> *'O L*ORD *God of our fathers, are you not God in heaven, and do You not rule over all the kingdoms of the nations, and in Your hand is there not power and might, so that no one is able to withstand You?'* (2 Chronicles 20:6)

In a time of crisis for his nation, Jehoshaphat called upon the covenant-keeping, sovereign Lord of the nations. In prayer he claimed the promises God had made to Solomon at the dedication of the temple (1 Kings 8:33, 34, 37, 38), namely that when an enemy sought to besiege the nation, if the people, or any individual from among them, went to the temple and called out to God, He would hear them. This is exactly what Jehoshaphat did. Acknowledging the greater strength of the enemy he claimed the covenant promise. And God kept His covenant and defeated the enemy without one blow of the sword. God's word will not return to Him void. In spite of what we see going on around us, we must pray and God will keep His word to subdue all nations. Praying the promises of our covenant in essence says to God, 'Our enemies are greater than us but our eyes are on you.'

Please note that the promise is not the same as the possession of the promise. The promise must be acted upon before it can become a possession. God promised that, after seventy years, Israel would return to Jerusalem from exile. However, if it was not for Daniel praying in the promise God had made through Jeremiah, the Jews may not ever have possessed Jerusalem again. Daniel prayed in the promise until it was possessed. We must do the same. We must pray, 'Your kingdom come' until it comes in totality. We must pray that God will keep His covenant and bring His bride out of every nation.

We have a God who does not slumber. In fact, the Son of God who established the everlasting covenant with His blood, *'lives to make intercession for them'* (Hebrews 7:25). I would imagine that He is praying that we will use the spiritual authority He has given us through prayer to take authority over Satan and his kingdom of darkness, making

the enemy His footstool (Hebrews 10:13). He desires that we
will pray to Him as 'the Lord of the harvest,' so that He will
dispatch empowered laborers into the harvest (Matthew
9:37–38).

We are not alone in our prayers. Though it is not reported
in Genesis 24, I cannot imagine that Abraham and Isaac were
not also praying. Eliezer knew of God's covenant with
Abraham and appealed to God on the basis of that covenant:

> 'O Lord God of my master Abraham, please give me success
> this day, and show kindness to my master Abraham.'
> (Genesis 24:12)

We, too, petition Father God to grant us success to save those
who will make up the bride of Christ. The covenant of
Abraham is still in effect, because it is included within the
greater covenant made through the blood of Jesus Christ. We
appeal to God based on the will created through the death of
Jesus Christ. Jesus said that if we ask anything according to
His will, through His name, it will be done for us (John
14:14). We know for sure that the will of God is in the very
word of God. The scriptures, such as those to which we have
previously eluded and others, are the basis of our appeal to
God. For instance, in the same way that God promised
Abraham that He would send an angel before his servant to
bring him success, so we too have the promise of angelic
intervention to help us in our mission to bring home a bride.

Angels are ministering agents to the heirs of salvation
(Hebrews 1:14). We can appeal to God to send angels ahead
of us to prepare people to hear the message of salvation.
According to Psalm 103:20, the angels obey the word of the
Lord. The God who wishes none to perish will certainly send
His angels ahead of us.

The servant prayed for a divine appointment:

> 'Behold, here I stand by the well of water; and the daughters
> of the men of the city are coming out to draw water. Now let
> it be that the young woman to whom I say, "Please let down
> your pitcher that I may drink," and she says, "Drink, and I
> will also give your camels a drink" – let her be the one You

*have appointed for Your servant Isaac. And by this I will
know that You have shown kindness to my master." '*
(Genesis 24:13–14)

We too should pray daily for God supernaturally to guide
people into our path based on His promise to build His
Church (Matthew 16:18).

Not only did the servant pray for a divine appointment, he
expected God to answer his prayer immediately.

*'And it happened, before he had finished speaking to the Lord
... that Rebekah ... came out ... And the servant ran to
meet her...'* (Genesis 24:15, 17)

Our lives and world would change if we would fervently pray
for and expect divine appointments. God desires to give us
divine appointments daily. Since all of history is based on
the redemption of the human race we can confidently and
expectantly look for God to orchestrate rendezvous with
those He longs to bring to Himself.

Steve Taylor, a Youth for Christ leader, brought together
most of the youth pastors in his area and challenged them to
plant a 'praying church' on each one of the thirty-six high
school campuses in Santa Clara County, California. By the
beginning of 1994 they had succeeded, and today more than
a thousand high school students have joined one of the
thirty-six 'congregations' which make up the Church on
Campus. The students are now being trained by Taylor and
his associates to pray before school and during class breaks
three specific prayers: the first one is for themselves; the
second one is a prayer for at least three fellow Christians on
campus; and the last one is a prayer for ten unsaved students
and three teachers. This equals more than 20,000 daily
prayers being lifted up on the high school campuses of Santa
Clara County. [2] Not only will students and teachers be saved,
but thousands of young teenagers are having a fresh, vital
experience with God daily as they pray expectantly.

A divine appointment prayer asks God to send ministering
angels before you to prepare those who will cross your path
that day. It asks the Holy Spirit to keep you sensitive to His

prompting, to be aware of needs around you, and share with those who have ears to hear. Such prayers believe God is ready to introduce us routinely to those who need His healing, delivering and saving touch.

Canadian theologian Dr Clark Pinnock writes:

> 'Brothers and sisters, our risen Lord has triumphed over the powers of evil. He now reigns at God's right hand, having all authority on heaven and earth. King Jesus now wills to save and heal human beings in every dimension of their fallen condition: in body, mind, and spirit ... Shall we not then exercise faith [through prayer] in the victorious power of Jesus to fight everything that enslaves and oppresses humankind? Shall we not take authority over all the power of the enemy? Shall we not determine to live our lives as those who expect miracles to come from the hand of God our Father – forsaking the paths of functional unbelief?' [3]

The New Testament Church believed that the covenant promises were to be fulfilled through them. They understood that the blood covenant made by Jesus Christ gave them the spiritual authority to pray for divine appointments and to see them fulfilled. John Robb points out that 'intercessory prayer is mentioned more than thirty times in the book of Acts alone,' and preceded virtually all 'major breakthroughs in the outward expansion of the early Christian movement.' [4]

What we need is that old-time religion that prays for divine appointments and expects the Savior to deliver them. Leonard Ravenhill has expressed the need very pungently:

> 'The church has many organizers, but few agonizers; many who pay, but few who pray; many resters, but few wrestlers; many who are enterprising, but few who are interceding. People who are not praying are playing.
>
> Two prerequisites of dynamic Christian living are vision and passion, and both of these are generated in the prayer closet. The ministry of preaching is open to a few. The ministry of praying is open to every child of God.

Do not mistake action for unction, commotion for
creation, and rattles for revivals.

The secret of praying is praying in secret. A worldly
Christian will stop praying and a praying Christian will
stop worldliness.

When we pray, God listens to our heartbeat.
Hannah's "lips" moved, but her voice was not heard
(1 Samuel 1:12, 13). When we pray in the Spirit, there
are groanings which cannot be uttered (Romans 8:26).

Tithes may build a church, but tears will give it life.
That is the difference between the modern church and
the early church. Our emphasis is on paying, theirs was
on praying. When we have paid, the place is taken.
When they had prayed, the place was shaken (Acts
4:31).

In the matter of effective praying, never have so many
left so much to so few. Brethren, let us pray.'

Church, be encouraged because George Otis Jr, in his book
Last of the Giants, reports that millions of believers are
obeying the stinging words of Leonard Ravenhill.

Happily, more Christians are praying today than ever
before. (This is undoubtedly one of the primary reasons for
the stunning success of global evangelisation over the past
several decades.) As of 1990, an estimated 170 million
persons across the planet were praying daily for world
mission. Twenty million of these were involved in full-time
prayer ministry, many as members of twenty active global
intercessory prayer networks or one of ten million weekly
prayer groups. [5]

Much of this renewed prayer emphasis is owed to the Holy
Spirit using prayer mobilizers such as: Paul Cedar, Chairman
of Mission America, President of the Evangelical Free
Church of America and Dean of the Billy Graham School of
Evangelism who has instilled thousands with a sense of awe
in God's presence as they gather in 'solemn assemblies';
David Bryant, who has organised Interdenominational
Concerts of Prayer, which have brought thousands together
to pray; Dr Joe Aldrich, President of Multnomah School of
the Bible, who is the vision behind thousands of 'Pastors'

Prayer Summits' which gather pastors from all walks to do nothing but pray for four days; Dr David Yonggi Cho, Pastor of the Yoido Full Gospel Church of Seoul, Korea, who has taught an entire generation of leaders about the necessity to pray at least three hours a day; Revelation Omar Cabrera, leader of a cluster of congregations numbering more than 80,000 members, who has taught the need for spiritual warfare through all-night prayer; Cindy Jacobs, who with her Generals of Intercession has marshaled prayer assaults in key parts of the world; C. Peter Wagner, Professor of Church Growth at Fuller Theological Seminary, who is the international coordinator of the most dynamic prayer ministry coalition ever assembled under the umbrella of the Prayer and Spiritual Warfare Track;[6] Dr Terry Tekyl, of Renewal Ministry, who is mobilising Methodist congregations to 'make room to pray,' instructing Methodist and other churches on how to set up and utilise 24-hour prayer rooms at their buildings.

The Moses, Aarons and Hurs are on the mountain praying with uplifted hands: it is time to release the Joshua Company to fight. As in the Gulf War, the air assault has led the way. Now, the ground attack will claim the final victory. The Holy Spirit is once again releasing earth-quaking prayers through His saints. We must now be ready for God to answer with divine appointments.

Study questions

1. What promises did God make to Abraham when He established His covenant with him? Have those promises been fulfilled?

2. Can we claim the Abrahamic Covenant today through prayer?

3. Can you list other scriptures that promise God will receive the glory He deserves from nations, kings and cities?

4. What is the difference between the promise and the possession of the promise? What action on our part is necessary to ensure the promise is possessed?

5. Do you believe praying these promises is important when interceding for those who do not yet know Christ? Why or why not?

6. Have you ever prayed in this manner when praying for the lost? If so, what were the results?

7. Have you ever asked God to give His angels a charge to minister to a person lost without Christ? Why or why not?

8. The servant prayed for a divine appointment. He prayed specifically and God answered specifically and immediately. Make a commitment to pray every morning for God to give you a divine appointment for that day. Use some of the scriptures that speak of God's promise to save the peoples (found in this chapter) or use one you are more familiar with. Ask the Lord to give His angels to those you will meet, preparing them before they meet you. Ask the Lord to help you to live and walk by His Spirit (Galatians 5:25). Return next week with your testimony.

Notes

1. Andrew Murray, *The Believers' New Covenant* (Minneapolis: Bethany House, 1984), pp. 13–14.

2. Ed Silvoso, *That None Should Perish: How to Reach Entire Cities for Christ Through Prayer Evangelism* (Ventura: Regal Books, 1994), p. 247.

3. George Otis Jr, *The Last of the Giants* (Tarry Town: Chosen Books, 1991), p. 248.

4. John Robb, 'Prayer as a Strategic Weapon in Frontier Missions,' *Society for Frontier Missiology* (13–15 September 1990).

5. Otis, *The Last of the Giants*, p. 248.

6. Silvoso, *That None Should Perish*, pp. 13–15.

Chapter 12

Divine Appointments

'And it happened, before he had finished speaking,
that behold, Rebekah ... came out...'
(Genesis 24:15)

'As for me, being on the way, the Lord led me
to the house of my master's brethren.'
(Genesis 24:27)

Divine appointments played a key role in leading Andrew Merely to Jesus, as he explains:

'Born into a Christian family, I was raised in Melbourne, Australia, attending a private school and as a part of a growing, family Baptist church.

By the age of 15, I was rebellious and only went to church occasionally to keep in contact with the girls. My life began to center on my own wants even though I made a commitment to the Lord at the age of 13.

By the time I left school, sports and parties were a big part of my life and up until the age of 28, this remained the case. Alcohol was also prominent and so when I decided to take a year off my job as a schoolteacher to travel around the world, the send off involved a lot of heavy drinking.

I decided to travel to the US. My mother weeping over my departure saying, "Someone is watching over you." But who is He? And how will I get to know Him? My adventure to salvation began at the same time as my trip around the world.

It didn't take long for God to catch my attention again. He did it through an attractive young lady who sat behind me on the plane from Hawaii to San Francisco. We got on well and I later visited her for a week in San Diego.

She was a brand new Christian and as I was very forward with women, by the end of the week she was happy to see me leave. But ... she had been used by God to further challenge me and I left an address and phone number to contact me in England so I could return her hospitality she had shown me in California.

I began hitchhiking throughout the USA and Canada. God continued to use Christians, ministers and even films to keep me searching for His reality. Just outside Houston, I stood on the side of the road holding a sign saying "Australian" and a car pulled over about 100 miles up the road. It reversed back and I saw an Asian-looking guy driving.

We got on quite well as I was a Physical Education teacher and he worked in the fitness industry and at the time was running an aerobics gym in Houston. His name was Doug Stringer.

Doug offered to put me up for the night which was not unusual in America, which is full of very friendly people. He took me to his aerobics studio and I thought that I had walked into a group of moonies – people hugged each other and called each brother and sister. I was relieved to find out that they were Christians and that the aerobics studio doubled as a ministry called Turning Point Ministries.

In Doug and the people at Turning Point, I saw the reality of the love of Jesus Christ – they cared for the people no one else cared for, they gave time, money and efforts for people who never intended returning anything.

What I saw lined up with their message that Jesus changed their lives and He was the reason they could and would love unconditionally. This was what I had been searching for.

At one of the meetings at the Turning Point aerobics studio in Houston in April, 1983, I asked God to forgive me for my rebellion and I made Jesus Lord of my life.

After being discipled by Doug, I left Houston and traveled to England via Washington, Boston and New York. In England, I got a phone call from Lynette, the Christian girl I last saw in San Diego. She nearly died of shock when I told her I had been born again but she was delighted. We hitchhiked around Scotland together and became close friends. We eventually parted for a time, meeting again in Italy when we realized our relationship had deepened.

About 18 months after we first met on the plane in Hawaii, Lynette and I were married in Australia. Eleven wonderful years and three beautiful children later, we have a marriage which is the backbone of our ministry.' [1]

Lynette, Doug Stringer and the countless Christians Andrew Merely met on his search were all divine appointments. They were all appointed by God to point Andrew towards Jesus Christ, his Savior. There are Andrew Merelys in our life every day. We may not recognise them as readily because we do not often see the end-result of our witness, as Doug Stringer and Lynette did with Andrew. Yet, all the points of contact played a significant role in Andrew continuing his search for unconditional love in Jesus Christ.

The servant Eliezer prayed for something very particular to happen that would confirm who the bride for Isaac should be. Behind this prayer was a confidence that God had appointed and prepared the right woman.

As we read God's Word, we come to the conclusion that God divinely arranges meetings and circumstances. There are many stories of people He appointed to influential positions for the salvation of His people (e.g. Moses, Samuel, Joseph, Daniel). Jesus Christ came in *'the fullness of time'* or the right time (Galatians 4:4). He had divine appointments with people, such as the woman at the well (John 4), Zacchaeus

(Luke 19:1–10), Bartimaeus (Mark 10:46–52), and others. Peter and John had a divine appointment with the lame man at the temple gate in Jerusalem (Acts 3:1–10), and Paul had a divine appointment with the twelve disciples at Ephesus (Acts 19:1–7). God has appointed times and seasons for deliverance and salvation. In fact, one reason for Jerusalem's destruction was because the Jews *'did not recognize the time of God's coming'* (Luke 19:14 NIV).

The Word tells us there are seasons or windows of opportunity for people to be saved:

> *'The harvest is past,*
> *The summer is ended,*
> *And we are not saved!'*   (Jeremiah 8:20)

> *'Also, O Judah, a harvest is appointed for you ... '*
> (Hosea 6:11)

God has appointed for human beings to die once and then to be judged (Hebrews 9:27). He has appointed a judge and a judgement day (Acts 17:31). But God's chief desire is to give life more abundantly; He does not desire the death of the wicked. Therefore, God does all He can to ensure that they receive life while they are on this earth. He wishes none to perish but all to come to repentance (2 Peter 3:9).

Because of His great desire to save people, God divinely arranges for His servants to be among His people for an appointed time to preach the good news of the gospel. It is important for us to know that the God who arranged for Jonah to preach to Nineveh, also seeks to give us divine appointments to preach the salvation of Jesus Christ. John Wimber's definition of a divine appointment was:

> '[A]n appointed time in which God reveals Himself to an individual or group through spiritual gifts or other supernatural phenomena. God arranges these encounters – they are meetings He had ordained to demonstrate His kingdom (Ephesians 2:10). The term "supernatural phenomena" includes specific answers to prayers for divine appointments through the individual

and others who have prayed and God's sovereign acts of mercy.'[2]

As is clear from 2 Corinthians 6:1, God intends the Church to take advantage of this period of grace. Jesus said,

> *'The harvest truly is plentiful, but the laborers are few. Therefore pray the Lord of the harvest to send out laborers into His harvest.'* (Matthew 9:37–8)

Pray that the Lord of Harvest will arrange for His servants to be in the harvest fields.

If you are walking in faith and in the will of God, you can confidently know that God has arranged for you to be in your current job, school, or neighborhood because there is a field of people ready to be harvested for God's kingdom. Frankly, even if you are not in God's perfect will, God is a master-weaver and He takes our wrong decisions and weaves them back into His plan. He will use you right where you are. I am not advocating missing God's perfect will – we have all missed it at some point in our lives – but I want those of you who may be missing it now to know that God will still arrange for you to meet with those who need our Savior.

If we are confident we are where God wants us to be, we especially need to be praying that God would bring people across our path. The God who desires to have communion with His bride will answer that prayer. Pastor Ron Walborn of the Christian Missionary Alliance gives an example of God answering such a prayer:

> 'Whenever I go to a person's house, to a sporting event or to other activities, I pray this prayer, "Lord, show me who you have prepared to receive the message of your kingdom in this place." One Saturday while waiting in a lift line at a ski resort in the Poconos, I prayed this prayer. Almost immediately I heard a young man, at least five people behind me in line, cursing and swearing. As I listened to his abusive language, the Spirit of God spoke, instructing me to witness to the teenager.

I quickly told God how impossible this would be since there were four people between us. As I said this, all four people dropped out of line, and the young man and I boarded the chair lift together. Not wanting to argue with the Lord any longer, I began to share about having a relationship with Jesus. As I spoke, tears began to fill the teen's eyes. He said that he had been dating the daughter of a preacher for three months, and that she had been sharing Jesus with him on a regular basis. As we neared the top of the mountain, he said through his tears, "I want to have a relationship with Jesus, too."'[3]

You too can see divine appointments happen on a daily basis. At your workplace, at the supermarket, ball game, Laundromat, or wherever you happen to be. We need to recognise divine appointments that come as a result of people's needs. Often, the physical, mental or emotional needs are the surface problems pointing to the root cause – their separation from God through sin. God arranges for you to be in relationship with such people for times when these needs arise. Often, the need produces power-encounters that demonstrate the kingdom's presence and the King's love. In his book *One-to-One* Pastor Terry Wardle recounts the story of one such occasion:

'You need to courageously step out in faith to pray for non-Christians. God will often demonstrate His power by meeting needs in their lives. Such "power encounters" verify that the kingdom of God is real and greater than the kingdom of darkness. Take Pat for example. A Spirit-filled Christian woman serving in a New England Church. One day she called Dorothy, an unbeliever, to chat on the phone. Dorothy expressed to Pat that she had a very bad sprain and was unable to put any weight on her ankle. Pat wanted to pray for her right then, but did not quite have the courage to do it. Instead, she simply told Dorothy she would be praying for her and hung up.

A short time later, while Pat was praying for Dorothy, she received a phone call. Dorothy was calling to say that the pain in her ankle had just stopped and that she could walk perfectly. This happened on a Thursday and, on the following Tuesday, Dorothy went to the home fellowship group Pat attends. During the ministry time, a woman asked for prayer for an inner ear problem that made her dizzy. People gathered around her to pray, and she was instantly healed.

Dorothy witnessed this dramatic work of the Holy Spirit. As a result of her own healing and of the one she had just witnessed, Dorothy accepted the Lord that night.

God is anxious to use Spirit-filled friendship evangelists in just this way. You should pray not only for healing, but for financial needs, marital problems and other life crises. This gives the Holy Spirit the opportunity to manifest His power in the face of darkness.' [4]

God's goodness will often bring repentance. Be careful to use the encounter to share the gospel and bring repentance based on the individual's lost condition and the Savior's compelling sacrifice on the cross to bring salvation.

If divine appointments can be experienced on a daily basis, our daily prayer should reflect this and we should be ready to act as God answers these prayers daily. Pray that God will put people in your path who need to see His power and love revealed to them. The Lord of the harvest will answer such a prayer.

Because He will give us these opportunities, we need our feet *'shod with the preparation of the gospel of peace'* (Ephesians 6:15). We need to *'be ready to give a defense to everyone who asks you a reason for the hope that is you'* (1 Peter 3:15), and we will *'walk in wisdom toward those who are outside, redeeming the time'* (Colossians 4:5). According to Proverbs 11:30 he who is wise wins souls. Acting with the wisdom of God will win souls. As circumstances arise that provide an opportunity to witness, those who are ready will receive wisdom from God and will act wisely to see the lost friend saved. God will give wisdom liberally because those asking have no doubt that God wants to save people.

Our servant thanked God after meeting Rebekah for his success and then prayed, *'As for me, being on the way...'*

(Genesis 24:27), meaning he was on his way doing God's will. This is how God leads us. We first put ourselves on God's way. A life that is disposed to God is one that allows Jesus to orchestrate people and events enabling us to share or demonstrate the gospel.

Just because your appointee does not respond positively does not mean it was not a divine appointment. Jesus had a divine appointment with the rich young ruler, yet *'he went away sorrowful, for he had great possessions'* (Mark 10:22).

One night as I was witnessing with others outside the Dixie Chicken bar in College Station, Texas, several Punkers approached and set out to make sport of us. Being from Texas A and M University, they were filled with all kinds of knowledge and challenged us about creation quoting Carbon-14 experiments. Even though we shared many examples of why Carbon-14 tests were not reliable and the evolution theory merely another unscientific religion, they did not listen and left scoffing. We felt pretty much like failures that evening. However, about a week later, one of the young men left a message on our answering machine saying, 'This tract says, "If your life needs changing, call." Well, I'm calling and you're not there. Call me back. I need help.' We were able to contact him and led him to Christ. The Word of God is powerful and penetrating.

In Genesis 24, after praying for a divine appointment, the servant runs to meet the first young woman he sees approaching the well. He had prayed for a divine appointment and expected God to answer that prayer. Then, he put feet to his faith. Someone once said, 'If you pray for rain, bring an umbrella.' Many pray for God to open up doors, but then sit back and wait for nothing to happen. God answers prayers that are accompanied with **faith** that has feet.

The Lord showed my wife how doors actually open when she was shopping and went into a store that had automatic sliding doors. She got about two feet from the door, stepped on the rubber mat and then the door opened. In the same way, we need to put feet to our prayer of faith in order for God to open a door for us. If you pray for God to bring divine appointments or open doors for you to share the gospel, you need to make yourself available. You need to engage in conversations at work; you need to reach out to your neighbor.

My wife and I were going through an all time low in our ministry life. Financially, we had made some mistakes and needed to take second jobs to support ourselves and the ministry. I picked up a job selling memberships at a local fitness center. The fleshly wear, attitudes and music made me make sure I was prayed up daily as I entered my new mission field. I also prayed for divine appointments because daily someone new would walk through the door looking to get fit. Of course, most were way out of shape spiritually as well. I would take the prospective member on 'the tour' during which I would ask probing questions looking for the Holy Spirit to give an opening to share the gospel. Many people were coming to find physical exertion or to get physically fit to bury a recent hurt or overcome inferiority and insecurity. In other words, they had come in with a spiritual need that only Jesus could meet. Several times as the tour ended in my office, I was able to share the gospel and bring them to Christ. The owners, being Christian, allowed me to baptise them immediately in the Jacuzzi.

The Jacuzzi was glass enclosed so those exercising were able to witness the baptisms. As we entered the wet area singing, the gym stopped and watched the baptism. Eventually, twelve people came to Christ during my employment at the gym. These divine appointments would not have occurred if the prayer of faith had not taken on feet and if I had not been willing to be available.

On my most recent trip to Nigeria, I visited one of our missionaries working among the unreached Ijaw people who live along the southern rivers of Nigeria. As I entered the central village of Ajakrama, many Nigerians met me and led me to a home. Our missionary Wilson Okotie was not around, nor were any of his disciples, so I took it that he had instructed the young men to accommodate me at this particular home. Wilson finally showed and informed me that I was in the wrong house; he had made other arrangements. But this was not just anyone's house: we were in the home of Chief Omawei, who was the most affluent chief in the area. He had personally funded the construction of the building for the cult that dominates the Ijaws. Leaving the chief's home would have been a big mistake. We decided God must be up to something, and I stayed with the chief that weekend. He attended every meeting I held and he appeared to be taking in what was being said. On the last day, I spent the afternoon with him and through a translator was able to discuss the teachings with him. He told me that several of his children had died and they did not know the cause. He had seen through the teaching that his cultic religion was in error and he wanted to become a Christian. He thoroughly repented and confessed Christ. Together we began to break the curse of death over his family and pleaded protection through the blood of Jesus. Before going home to be with Jesus, Chief Omawei went with Missionary Wilson Okotie on the village outreaches and gave a home, a boat and a building to use for training new converts. He was used to coming to the defense of Wilson, who was brought before the King on charges of converting the cult members and disturbing the gods of Igbesu through his all-night prayer meetings. After hearing the chief's testimony, the King welcomed Missionary Wilson to stay.

A heavenly arrangement was made the day I entered the village of Ajakrama. I, like the servant in our story, can testify *'As for me, being on the way, the Lord led me to the house...'* of Chief Omawei. The Lord will lead you, too, as you are on the way.

Study questions

1. Recount a divine appointment you have had personally.

2. Give your definition of a divine appointment.

3. Can you recall a divine appointment in the Gospels or in the book of Acts?

4. Why do you think it is important to pray and look for divine appointments? Do you agree that there are windows of opportunity for people to be saved (cf. Jeremiah 8:20; Hosea 6:11)?

5. Divine appointments often come through people's needs. Discuss some of those needs and how we can be used to meet them as a means to share Christ.

6. The servant's prayer, *'As for me, being on the way...'*, is indicative of an attitude we need in order to be used in divine appointments. What is it?

7. Have you experienced what you thought was a divine appointment, only to see the appointee not get saved? Describe the event. Do you now believe it was divine?

Notes

1. 'Testimony of Andrew Merely,' provided by Doug Stringer, Turning Point Ministries, Houston, Texas.

2. John Wimber, *Power Evangelism* (San Francisco: Harper and Row, 1986), p. 51.

3. Terry Wardle, *One-to-One* (Camphill: Christian Publications, 1989), p. 104.

4. *Ibid*, p. 105.

Chapter 13

Where Are the People of Passion?

'And the servant ran to meet her, and said,
"Please let me drink a little water from your pitcher."'
(Genesis 24:17)

Where are the people of passion?

The servant's passion for his master dictated his actions as he attempted to bring home a bride for the master's son. The servant's passion is demonstrated when he sees the young woman approaching the well and his faith takes feet and he runs. The compassion of God runs after sinners. In the parable of the prodigal son, Luke reports,

> *'But when he* [the son] *was still a great way off, his father saw him and had compassion for him, and ran and fell on his neck...'* (Luke 15:20)

Catherine Booth, who with her husband founded the Salvation Army which brought thousands from the streets of England to Christ, wrote:

> 'Oh, people say you must be very cautious. You must not push religion down people's throats. What?! Should I wait until an unconverted, godless man wants to be saved before I try to save him? Am I to let my unconverted friends and acquaintances go quietly down to damnation and never tell them about their souls until they ask, "If you please, I want you to preach to me." Is

this anything like the spirit of early Christianity? No! Therefore you must make them look and if they run from you in one place, meet them in another and let them have no peace until they submit to God. This is what Christianity ought to be doing in this land, and there are plenty of Christians around to do it. Why, we might give the world such a time of it that they would get saved in self-defense. If we were only aggressive enough and determined that they should have no peace in their sins.' [1]

Where are people of such passion today? The Booths had a passion for God and this brought a compassion for souls. They ran and captured thousands for Christ.

Missionary J. Hudson Taylor was known as 'God's Man in China' because he won so many Chinese to Christ. This story, from his biography, tells of his passion/compassion that earned him his title before he ever went to China:

'The unsaved at home were just as much a burden on his heart as the unsaved in China. Always and everywhere he was a soul-winner.

One of his employer's patients had been a hard drinker, and now in middle life was suffering from senile gangrene. His condition was serious and his hatred of everything to do with religion so intense that it seemed hopeless to try to influence him. Hudson Taylor wrote:

"The disease commenced as usual insidiously, and the patient had little idea that he was a doomed man and probably had not long to live. I was not the first to attend him, but when the case was transferred to me I became very anxious about his soul. The family with whom he lived were Christians, and from them I learned that he was an avowed atheist and very antagonistic to anything religious. They had without asking his consent invited a Scripture Reader to visit him, but in great passion he had ordered him from the room. The vicar of the district had also called, hoping to help him, but he had spat in his face and refused to allow him to speak. His temper was described to be as very violent, and altogether the case seemed as hopeless as could well be imagined.

Upon first commencing to attend him I prayed much about it, but for two or three days said nothing of a religious nature. By special care in dressing his diseased limb I was able considerably to lessen his sufferings, and he soon began to manifest appreciation of my services. One day with a trembling heart I took advantage of his grateful acknowledgements to tell him what was the spring of my action, and to speak of his solemn position and need of God's mercy through Christ. It was evidently only a powerful effort of self-restraint that kept his lips closed. He turned over in bed with his back to me, and uttered no word.

I could not get the poor man out of my mind, and very often through each day I pleaded with God, by His Spirit, to save him ere He took him hence. After dressing the wound and relieving the pain, I never failed to say a few words to him which I hoped the Lord would bless. He always turned his back looking annoyed, but never made any reply.

After continuing this for some time my heart sank. It seemed to me that I was not only doing no good but perhaps really hardening him and increasing his guilt. One day after dressing his limb and washing my hands, instead of returning to the bedside I went to the door and stood hesitating a moment with the thought in my mind, 'Ephraim is joined to his idols, let him alone'. Looking at my patient I saw his surprise as it was the first time since opening the subject that I had attempted to leave without saying a few words for my Master.

I could bear it no longer. Bursting into tears, I crossed the room and said: 'My friend, whether you will hear or whether you will forbear, I must deliver my soul,' and went on to speak very earnestly, telling him how much I wished that he would let me pray with him. To my unspeakable joy he did not turn away, but replied: 'If it will be a relief to you, do.' I need scarcely say that falling upon my knees I poured out my soul to God on his behalf. Then and there, I believe, the Lord wrought a change in his soul. He was never afterwards unwilling to be spoken to and prayed with, and within a few days he definitely accepted Christ as his Savior.

The now happy sufferer lived for some time after this change, and was never tired of bearing testimony to the grace of God. Though his condition was most distressing the alteration in his character and behavior made the previously painful duty of attending him one of real pleasure, I have often thought since in connection with this case and the work of God generally of the words, 'He that goeth forth and weepeth, bearing precious seed, shall doubtless come again with rejoicing, bringing his sheaves with him.' Perhaps if there were more of that intense distress for souls that leads to tears, we should more frequently see the results we desire. Sometimes it may be that while we are complaining of the hardness of the hearts of those we are seeking to benefit, the hardness of our own hearts and our own feeble apprehension of the solemn reality of eternal things may be the true cause of our want of success.'' [2]

Passion for God caused Hudson Taylor to run after this sinner. Compassion for souls caused him to weep over the lost state of his patient. The compassion for God that weeps over sinners broke the man's stony heart. If God were to run an ad for employees, it would read: 'Wanted: Weeping Workers. No experience necessary.'

Nehemiah and Jeremiah wept over the sins of the people and their forefathers; David wept over his enemy King Saul; Jesus wept over the city of Jerusalem which rejected and crucified Him. We will sow in tears before we reap with joy.

After much toil in our efforts to save lost friends, relatives and acquaintances with seemingly no results we have a tendency to give up. God is interested in breaking our hearts before He breaks theirs. God is not merely after a soul, He is interested in developing the hearts of soul winners.

'I am a brokenhearted man,' confessed the outstanding Wesleyan preacher John Smith. 'Not for myself, but on account of others: my God has given me such a sight of the value of precious souls, that I cannot live if souls are not saved. Oh, give me souls, or else I die.'[3] Of compassion, J.H. Jowett said, 'Tearless hearts can never be the heralds of passion. We must pity if we would redeem. We must bleed if we would be ministers of the saving blood.'[4] Dick Eastman commented, 'Indeed one can never underestimate the power of brokenness before the Lord. It is unfortunate that much of our praying is devoid of deep-felt compassion. This is especially regrettable since nothing seems to hold more power in touching God than a broken spirit.'[5]

The passion for God that leads to a compassion for souls will have power. As our Savior knew, bearing witness for Him could not be done without it. He tells the frightened disciples to stay in Jerusalem and wait for the endowment of power from on high. It takes power to develop character that will make you a credible herald of the gospel and make the message effective. It takes power to overcome insecurities, inferiorities and fears. Paul came in weakness, fear and much trembling but his passion for God and compassion for the lost brought the power of God which overcame all his human frailties (1 Corinthians 2:1–5).

The servant did not fear losing face, reputation, or image. He did not think, 'What if I'm mistaken and she's not the one? I'll appear so foolish.' In fact, he seemed unconscious of himself altogether as he ran without caution up to the young woman.

The servant had a passion – he wanted to please his master and see Isaac have the love of his life. He was oblivious to anything else. This love for God and compassion for sinners will empower us to drive away all fears. Since passion for God and compassion for humanity is a condition of the heart that every believer is to have, we have no excuse for our 'guilty silence.' God will see and hear our passion for Him and His creation. The Holy Spirit will pour out power enabling us to overcome the fears that seek to muzzle us.

Someone said to James Farmer, former Director of the Commission on Racial Equality, 'What do you want from me? I'm just an innocent bystander.' Farmer answered, 'If you are a bystander, you are not innocent.'[6] If we are bystanders we are not innocent. We are guilty. Guilty of a lack of passion for God and compassion for people, for these qualities would move God to send His power to get our feet and lips moving to His glory.

> Could a mariner sit idle if he heard the drowning cry?
> Could a doctor sit in comfort and just let his patients die?
> Could a fireman sit idle, let men burn and give no hand?
> Can you sit at ease in Zion, with unreached peoples damned? [7]

Are you a person of passion?

Study questions

1. Name a Bible character whom you think had passion. Give your reasons for your view.

2. Explain how a passion for God will give us a compassion for people.

3. Have you ever run after a sinner? If yes, describe what happened.

4. Reread the last paragraph from Hudson Taylor's biography on p. 134. Has the hardness of the hearts of those who do not know Christ ever brought the hardness of your own heart to breaking and then bursting for tears?

5. Have you ever wept for the soul of someone or some group and then seen those sown tears reap a harvest? If so, explain what happened. If not, think about whether or not you believe it is an indication of your spiritual condition.

6. Name several benefits (mentioned in this chapter and others you might think of) that a passion for God and a compassion for the lost will bring.

7. Can a passion for Christ be developed? How might you go about it?

8. Is it possible to have a passion for God and not demonstrate compassion for those lost without Christ. Give reasons.

9. Write out a specific course of action for this week to develop or strengthen your passion for God.

10. Write out your plans to exhibit a compassion for those in need of God.

Notes

1. Catherine Booth, 'Aggressive Christianity,' Last Days Ministries, the author's personal collection.

2. Dr and Mrs Taylor Howard, *J. Hudson Taylor – God's Man in China: A Biography* (Chicago: Moody, 1987), pp. 49–50.

3. Dick Eastman, *Change the World School of Prayer: Basic Manual* (Mission Hills, CA, 1983), p. 85.

4. *Ibid.*, p. 85.

5. *Ibid.*, p. 85.

6. Norman Lewis, *Priority One: What God Wants* (Orange: Promise, 1988), p. 73.

7. *Ibid.*, p. 100.

Chapter 14

'And He Worshipped'

'Then the man bowed down his head, and worshipped the
Lord. And he said, "Blessed be the Lord God of my master
Abraham, who has not forsaken His mercy and His truth
toward my master. As for me, being on the way, the Lord led
me to the house of my master's brethren." '
(Genesis 24:26–27)

In his success, the selfless servant gives the most striking
example of what the Church ought to be. After each step of
success, the servant *'bowed down his head and worshipped'*
(Genesis 24:26, 52). The times when we are most tempted to
forget God are not periods of despair, but of prosperity and
success. For this reason Paul cautioned his readers,

> *'But I discipline my body and bring it into subjection: lest,*
> *when I have preached to others, I myself should become*
> *disqualified.'*   (1 Corinthians 9:27)

It was after David finally succeeded in becoming king that
he fell into adultery with Bathsheba. Sexual promiscuity was
only the surface cause of a deeper root problem that had
sprung up in David's heart as a result of his success – **pride**.
David's sin of passion was in reality a sin of pride. Pride said,
'I deserve Bathsheba and want her and will have her.' On
another occasion the sin of pride in taking a census of his
people, when God had forbidden it, brought a plague that
killed 70,000 (see 2 Samuel 24). And today, God's servants are

still plagued with the pride that keeps count of God's victories. It is not as obvious today since we are much more sophisticated. We preface our reports with 'Give God the glory, 125 were saved today.' We are willing to give Him glory as long as the people were saved through us.

The servant truly worshipped God for his success. True worship is honoring God for who He is and what He has done. There is no sense of pride in this humble servant and his immediate act of worship kept his heart pure.

Soul winners must be true worshippers of God. Worshipping God defuses pride and keeps us humble. The literal meaning of the most common word used for worship illustrates this humble attitude. The Greek word for worship, προσκυνῶ (pros-koo-neh'-o), means 'to kiss towards or to prostrate oneself.' It is the picture of a peasant bringing the portion of the harvest he owes to his feudal Lord: as he lays his gifts before his throne, the King would stretch out his right hand with the signet ring and, without touching it, the peasant would kiss towards it in his honor.

Anything fruitful that comes from our life has originated in God. We lay all our crowns graciously before Him in worship and declare Him as the true owner of it all.

This is true evangelism. He is the Lord of the harvest. He is the Lord of hosts who is moving His angels to destroy our enemies, allowing us to go in and plunder the enemy's territory of souls held captive. With the great harvest of men and women being saved today, it is no coincidence that men who have a prophetic voice in our country have said the key element for leadership in our times is humility. God's power and ability is going to grace true worshippers with a harvest of men and women won for Him. In this last harvest, God will not give His glory to another (Isaiah 48:11).

The servant's worship demonstrated a sweet total dependence on God. Without God, how would the servant have known whom to pick as the bride? Where would the camels and proper gifts have come from if God had not blessed his master Abraham? We, like the servant, have nothing to offer God but our lives to be used in His work on earth. We are poor and without spiritual ability to accomplish anything. We can do nothing that will count in eternity without the help of Jesus Christ. Paul said, *'by the grace of God I am what I am'* (1 Corinthians 15:10). By the power and giftings of the Holy Spirit, Paul was who he was.

As witnesses for Christ, have we anything to offer in and of ourselves? Unless the Spirit endows us with His life and presence, no one will be saved. Worship recognises this and says, 'God, without you I cannot do it.' It is this worshipping witness that God uses. He uses those who declare themselves weak. As Paul said, *'having nothing, and yet possessing all things'* (2 Corinthians 6:10). We have no life in and of ourselves that could produce spiritual life in others but God gives us His life. We are given the words of life by Jesus Christ. As we speak, the Holy Spirit produces, and God *'gives the increase'* (1 Corinthians 3:7).

Hannah was a true worshipper of God. Hannah and Peninnah were the wives of Elkanah but while Peninnah possibly had up to ten sons, Hannah was barren (see 1 Samuel 1). As barrenness was looked upon as a curse from God, it was most trying for Hannah to go to Shiloh annually to worship. It must truly have been a sacrifice of praise from her lips. You can picture her tagging along behind as Peninnah struts into the temple at Shiloh like a proud peacock with her ten sons. Elkanah, sympathetic to his childless wife, would always give Hannah a greater portion to sacrifice. I suggest Elkanah represents our Lord. As we come to God, we say, 'Lord, I am barren and I have nothing to offer you, but here I am.' The Lord says, 'I do not love you because you produce. I love you for who you are. Here is a gift to use as a sacrifice for me.' God gives us gifts and abilities to be used as a loving sacrifice to Him.

The name Hannah means 'grace.' Hannah probably tried endlessly to become pregnant. She might have eaten certain foods that someone told her would make her more fertile. She probably examined every area of her sexual relationship with Elkanah because she so longed to produce.

Finally, her barrenness brought her to brokenness (1 Samuel 1:10). Broken over her inability to become fruitful, the brokenness led her to total dependence on God as the Lord of life (1 Samuel 1:11). If the Lord will give her a son, she vows to dedicate him to His service. When the child is born, she names him Samuel which means 'Because I asked him of the Lord,' revealing her dependence on the Lord's grace to give life.

If you have been an ardent worker in the harvest fields, you have probably experienced seasons of drought and barrenness where you saw little, if any, fruit of people being saved. Going to church, or better yet a pastor's conference, is a sacrifice of praise as your ministry peers ask the painful qualifying question, 'How many members are you running now, brother?' You have tried all the church growth methods of the 2,000 fastest-growing churches in America but none seem to work for you. Your barrenness brought or will bring you to brokenness. **You** cannot produce life. Your brokenness brings your heart to surrender to the Lordship of Jesus Christ in a deeper way. You declare to God that any sons and daughters that are won will honor and give Him glory. They are not yours, but His. God then graces you. His grace produces worship in you that declares your dependence on the God of your salvation (1 Samuel 2:1–10).

Worship gives honor to whom honor is due. If God gives life and the increase, no glory or honor should go to Apollos, Paul or Cephas. It is honor due only to God. The servant, Eliezer, was doing just that when he 'bowed down and worshipped.'

The donkey which Christ rode down the Mount of Olives, during what is known as the Triumphal Entry into Jerusalem, was asked by his fellow burrows how his day fared. 'Oh, it was a day like none other,' he said. 'A crowd met me at the top of Mount Olivet and led a procession of singing about me. They laid down blankets and palm trees before my path as if I were a king. Some even got so carried away as to make claims of deity. I had a great day.' It seems many of us are taking Jesus for a ride. We do ministry for God but are quick to receive the praise of men. The purpose of our lives is to glorify Him and Him alone. Those who are ready to lay down their titles and personal accolades for the testimony of Jesus will be used of God in these last days.

We are coming into the Davidic age of the Church. Saul killed his thousands but David killed his tens of thousands (1 Samuel 18:7). The Saul era was when big ministries and big money were idolised. Man and his ministry were lifted up. We can be thankful for the Saul era. People were saved and at times the kingdom advanced. But God is bringing that era down; in fact, it is dead.

Now, a new era has come. A remnant of ragtag worshippers have been trained in the school of obscurity. Lowly servants, who like David, love and worship God, and whose sole desire is to see the King and His kingdom come and His will be done: this is the type of person God will use mightily in these last days. Our Lord has prepared an army of them. Are you in this army?

As I have already pointed out, all life comes from God. Therefore, institutions, ministries and preachers are not the source, but only the channel of that life. The servant did not worship Abraham, but the God of Abraham.

'He who glories, let him glory in the Lord.'
(1 Corinthians 1:31)

'Therefore let no one boast in men.'   (1 Corinthians 3:21)

The Greek word for witness is μαρτυρεω (mar-too-ree'-o), from which we get our word 'martyr.' In order to be a witness, you must be ready to be martyred. You have to live as if you were dead and only alive to Christ. Though we may praise dead men, dead men cannot claim honor or praise for themselves – they are dead.

Taking the glory for oneself is like a man's son asking him for money to buy him a Christmas gift. He gives him the money, the boy buys the gift, gives it to him and proudly tells his friends what he gave his dad. This is childish but it is often how we act. God is seeking worshippers who worship in spirit and in truth. (He is seeking those who know the truth.) We have nothing to give to God unless the Spirit of God invests in us. If that little boy gives the gift to his dad and says, 'Thank you, Dad, for giving me the money to buy a gift for you. I love you and hope you like what I bought,' any father's heart would leap with gladness. This is what we say in worship. 'Jesus, I know anything I have You have given to

me, and I thank You. I pray that You are pleased with what I
have done with what You have given me.'

Our worship produces faith. Worship is thanking God for
what He has done. *'As for me,'* prayed the servant, *'being on
the way, the* LORD *led me to the house of my master's brethren.'*
The thanksgiving leads to a greater faith in God. It creates a
trust in what God will do.

As we sincerely thank God for His accomplishments
through our human frailty, our faith in what He will do in
the future increases. The worshipper, David, grew in his faith
after killing the lion and the bear and this enabled him to
tackle Goliath. On the other hand, the Israelites, in spite of
awesome wonders performed by the Lord, failed to have the
attitude of worship and gratitude. They grumbled and
complained until D-day came. The day they should have
entered victoriously into the Promised Land, instead turned
into a day of fear and shrinking back from their powerful
enemies. Just as thanksgiving feeds faith, ingratitude feeds
unbelief and doubt.

Thanksgiving gives you the eyes of faith. You look not to
your own abilities but to the God who cannot fail. Our faith
is in God and worshipping God in thanksgiving says, 'I
believe You are who You say You are. I believe You will do
what You say You will do.' The servant thanked the God of
Abraham for being gracious and being true to His promise.

Our witness is also worship! Another word used for
worship, λατρυω (lat-ryoo'-o), means 'a service rendered to
God.' Once we are in the habit of glorifying God in all we say,
our witnessing itself becomes worship.

No true worship is offered until the worshipper is
controlled by the Holy Spirit and is using the gifts of the
Spirit. When this happens, the very life of the believer can
described as a service of worship.[1] As you use your spiritual
gift (and all gifts can be used effectively in evangelism), you
are worshipping in spirit as you proclaim the truth of the
glorious gospel of our Lord, Jesus Christ. Our gifts are not
confined to a building, but are signs that are to accompany
those who go in the name of Christ. Therefore, neither is our
worship confined to a building on Sunday morning. Our
lives are to be living sacrifices through our daily witness of

the one who died for us. This is our reasonable worship (Romans 12:2). Witnessing will mean conflict, ridicule, and humiliation. As we share His love in the midst of a hostile world, we say with our lives, 'Jesus, I love you and honor you above my own reputation, my need to be liked and my very life.'

God inhabits the praises of His people. As God was praised in the temple, His glory filled it (2 Chronicles 5). You are that house of worship. As you worship through witnessing, expect God to be present. He is Emmanuel, 'God with us.' He will save His people from their sins through you. The Spirit of the Lord will rest upon you to set the captive free. God will be present and will glorify His Son, Jesus, through your worshipful witness.

Study questions

1. Can you recall a time when success led you to the sin of pride?

2. How would worship have kept you from that sin?

3. How have you specifically worshipped God for who He is? What has He been to you? Example: I worship God as Provider because He has supplied . . .

4. What does our worship say about us? About God?

5. Have you ever felt like Hannah? How did you come out of that time of barrenness?

6. Why is it silly for us to take any glory for any success we might enjoy? (See story of boy who bought his father a Christmas gift.)

7. How does our thanksgiving affect our faith? Name a time when you acknowledged God, thanked Him for His work in your life, and when it produced faith for your next step.

8. Have you ever thought of your witness as worship? Explain how your active witnessing can be worshipping in spirit and in truth.

Note

1. David Hesselgrave Jr, *Planting Churches Cross Culturally* (Grand Rapids: Baker Book House, 1980), p. 318.

Chapter 15

The True-value Meal

*'Food was set before him to eat, but he said, "**I will not eat,
until I have told about my errand.**"
And he said, "Speak on."'*
(Genesis 24:33)

As I have studied the Scriptures, I have found that when
people are in haste, sin is not too far behind. However, there
is one area in which God constantly wants us to feel a sense
of urgency – an urgency to see people saved. Life is short for
us earthlings, and therefore it is important to be saved while
there is still time, as the scriptures emphasise:

*'... it is appointed for men to die once, but after this the
judgment.'*   (Hebrews 9:27)

*'Seek the LORD while He may be found,
Call upon Him while He is near.'*   (Isaiah 55:6)

*'Thus says the LORD:
"In an acceptable time I have heard You,
And in the day of salvation I have helped You."'*
(Isaiah 49:8)

The matter is urgent: we need to be active in our mission to
win men and women to God. God keeps us in this place of
urgency by telling us that, although His return is certain, the
day of His return is not known.

'Watch therefore – give strict attention, be cautious and active for you do not know in what kind of day (whether a remote or near one) your Lord is coming.'
(Matthew 24:42 Amplified Bible)

Therefore, there is an urgency as the time grows shorter for the scriptural fulfillment of Christ's return. We need to live each day as if it was going to be our wedding day. Abraham's servant had this sense of urgency to see his promise to Abraham fulfilled before his master died.

Our sense of urgency to win the lost is increased, too, by the horrible reality of an eternal hell. Paul had a keen understanding of judgement and hell:

'For we must all appear before the judgment seat of Christ, that each one may receive the things done in the body, according to what he has done, whether good or bad. Knowing, therefore, the terror of the Lord, we persuade men; but we are well known to God, and I also trust are well known in your consciences.'   (2 Corinthians 5:10–11)

Jesus said, if your eye causes you to sin it is better for you to gouge it out and go through life blind than for your whole body and your soul to be cast into hell (Matthew 5:29). Jesus is not merely exaggerating to get people to take sin seriously: He is showing us the horrible reality of hell. For me, knowing the hell that Jesus passed through in His trial and crucifixion, so that we could escape hell's eternal pain, is enough to make me avoid it. Remember – hell is final: it has no parolees. There is no time off for good behavior. (See the parable of the rich man and Lazarus in Luke 16.) This is a message that still needs to be told. Once we have earned the right to speak, in a world where people do everything they can to avoid pain and suffering, a message of eternal darkness with gnashing of teeth (or major league pain) in hell may find an open ear.

But just as urgent is the message of heaven. God has prepared a place where there is no more crying, sorrow, or dying, where there are no light bills, the streets are paved with gold and everyone has a luxury apartment in a massive condo built by God. No one should miss out on heaven. The servant's message to Laban in order to obtain his consent to take Rebekah back as Isaac's bride was:

> 'The LORD *has blessed my master greatly, and he has become great; and He has given Him flocks and herds, silver and gold, male and female servants, and camels and donkeys.'*
> (Genesis 24:35)

This must have sounded like heaven to Laban. God does not wish any to perish: that is why He built a heavenly city for us (2 Peter 3:9; Hebrews 11:10).

Yet, missing heaven is not about missing a place but a **person**. What makes it heaven is that God is there. Jesus tells the story of a great banquet (see Luke 14). In the story the host sends his servants out to tell those who have been invited that the food is now ready, but his guests refuse to come. And so the servant is told to go to the poor, the lame, the blind, in the byways and along the country roads *'and urge and constrain them to yield and come in so that my house may be filled'* (Luke 14:23 Amplified Bible). Today, it would be like going to the poor in the USA and saying, 'The President is throwing a huge banquet in Madison Square Garden, but the turkeys he invited did not show so he told me to invite you.' 'The President of the US wants me?' 'Yeah, you can eat all you want.' I am sure the down-and-outs would enjoy the food, but the best thing would be the honor of being with the President. God invites us to His banqueting table. Jesus invites us to a love relationship as His bride. We do not want anyone to miss out.

For Abraham's servant the overriding urgency was for this God-ordained bride to be brought to her appointed husband and to live with him on father Abraham's thousand-acre ranch. Our urgency is due to the fact that the return of the bridegroom is imminent, and the time for people to receive the promise of salvation is short. Thousands pass daily into the horrific hell intended for the devil and his angels. Even unbelievers are aware that the sun is setting on the earth's existence as evidenced by the production of books and movies predicting the world's destruction. More than anything else, like Abraham's servant, it is our passion for our

Savior to have His bride and therefore our compassion for
people to be saved and enjoy life now and forever with Him
in heaven. This is our motivation, compelling us to go and
share the good news.

The servant's sense of urgency comes through at many
points in the story. In Genesis 24:31–33, we see that, after the
many miles of travelling, Laban offers the tired, hungry
servant a refreshing meal, but the servant refuses to eat until
he has discharged his business. Now, that is a sense of
urgency. Again, the servant does not think of himself, and
his tired old body and growling stomach. His only thought is
of his master's son needing a bride. The Church of Jesus
Christ in America lacks this urgency. Our main business here
on earth is not to enjoy fine foods and drive the fanciest of
cars. Our main business is to bring home a bride for the Lord
Jesus Christ.

In John 4, we see Jesus ministering to the Samaritan
woman at the well while the disciples are off in town buying
food. When they return they find Jesus in the middle of His
conversation. The woman rushes off to town, telling the
people to *'Come, see a Man who told me all things that I ever did!
Could this be the Christ?'* (John 4:29–30). Meanwhile, the
disciples urge Jesus to eat, but He responds,

> *'I have food to eat of which you do not know.'* (John 4:32)

What was this food? Was it some great mystery or deep
spiritual teaching? No. Jesus answers His own question,

> *'My food is to do the will of Him who sent Me, and to finish
> His work* [of redeeming humankind]. *Do you not say,
> "There are still four months and then comes the harvest?"
> Behold, I say to you, lift up your eyes, and look at the fields,
> for they are already white for harvest.'*   (John 4:34–35)

I want you to catch Jesus' vivid teaching skill. The question is
about physical nourishment and satisfaction, but Jesus is
obviously speaking of the spiritual nourishment and satisfaction that motivates Him but obviously not His disciples at
this point in time. He is nourished or motivated by His desire

to finish the redemptive work the Father began in Noah. He clarifies this by saying, 'The harvest is ready now.' As Jesus is speaking, He sees the Samaritans, whom the woman is bringing to meet Him, coming up the road. He points to the Samaritan crowd and says, 'This is your harvest field' (my paraphrase). As you can see, Jesus is teaching His disciples that His Church is a missionary Church. His Father's redemptive work is for all peoples.

This whole incident was an indictment on the lackluster spiritual life of the disciples. The disciples, who lived with Jesus, were preoccupied with filling their bellies. The Samaritan woman, who had only known Jesus for a few moments, went into the very same town and brought out its people to see Jesus.

There is a harvest field all around us. Do you see it? If you do see it, do you have that sense of urgency to bring others to see Jesus and drink of the living water? Are you nourished by the same food as Jesus? Or does the thought of proclaiming the good news of Jesus Christ give you indigestion? When was the last time you fasted for people to come to Christ? When was the last time you were so involved in ministering Christ to the lost that food didn't enter your thinking because your nourishment came from doing the work of Jesus Christ. Oftentimes this has been our privilege as we ministered in the streets here and in Nigeria. During those times, to have eaten would have been to miss out on the real meal. The true-value meal is in being a part of God's redemptive work in Christ. What Jesus told the disciples is also a stinging rebuke to us! We do not know about the food Jesus has to eat.

Gluttony makes us spiritual sluggards; we are drowsy and our spiritual eyes are made dull because of the god of our belly. The number of restaurants and the bombardment of food advertisements have made us a nation that lives to eat rather than eats to live. The Church has followed suit.

Fast and pray to recover your spiritual sight. Fast and pray to recover that sense of urgency to see the captives set free and liberty preached to the imprisoned. Fast and pray until you become broken over what breaks God's heart. (A good book on fasting is Arthur Wallis' *God's Chosen Fast*, included in the Suggested Reading selection at the end of this book.)

A prophet speaks not only the truth of God but the heart of God. The heart of zeal and urgency which God wants His Church to have until the work is accomplished, is evident in Isaiah 62:6–7:

> *'I have set watchmen on your walls, O Jerusalem;*
> ***They shall never hold their peace day or night.***
> ***You who make mention of the*** Lord, ***do not keep***
> ***silent,***
> ***And give Him*** [Jesus] ***no rest till He establishes***
> ***And till He makes Jerusalem a praise in the***
> ***earth.'***

Jesus says, hound me until it's done. Pester me with your prayers until I make Jerusalem an object of praise on the earth, until my kingdom comes and my will is done in every tribe, tongue and nation. Cry out until I build my Church worldwide.

Today many Christians are quoting Revelations 22:17, *'And the Spirit and the bride say, "Come."'* This verse is in the last chapter of the last book of the Bible. Therefore, before the bride can come, all the prophecy of Revelation has first to be fulfilled. This means that not until everyone that could be saved has been saved, will the Spirit and the bride (the Church) say, 'Come.' Until then, the Father and the Son have said, 'Go.' **The command of the Father and the Son, who say 'Go,' must be completely obeyed before the Spirit and the bride can say, 'Come.'**

The servant received the command of father Abraham and son Isaac to go and there was no stopping him – not for food, not for any personal desire – until he had brought home the bride. The servant had no peace until the bride was safe in the arms of the son of his master. His food was to finish the work for which his master had sent him.

Another man who knew the food Jesus ate and lived with an urgency for lost souls, was Keith Green. I'll close this chapter with the words from his song, 'Asleep in the Light':

Do you see, do you see/All the people sinking down?
Do not you care, do not you care?/Are you gonna' let
them drown?
God's calling and you're the one/How can you be so
numb?
You close your eyes and/Pretend your job's done.

'Oh bless me Lord, bless me Lord':/You know it's all I
ever hear
No one aches, no one hurts/No one even sheds a tear
But He cries, He weeps, He bleeds/And He cares for
your needs
And you just lay back and keep soaking it in/Can't you
see it's such a sin?

Cause He sends people to your door/And you turn
them away
While you smile and say/'God bless you, be at peace'
And all heaven just weeps/Cause Jesus came to your
door.

You've left Him out on the streets.
Open up, Open up/And give yourself away
You see the need, you hear the cry/So how can you
delay?
God's calling and you're the one/But like Jonah you
run
He's told you to speak/But you keep holding it in
Can't you see it's such a sin?

The world is sleeping in the dark/That the church just
can't fight
Cause it's asleep in the light/How can you be so dead,
When you have been so well fed?/Jesus rose from the
grave
You can't even get out of bed!/Jesus rose from the dead
Come on get out of your bed!

Do you see, do you see/All the people sinking down?
Do not you care, do not you care?/Are you gonna' let
them drown? [1]

Study questions

1. List some current events that make you more aware of the return of Christ and the world's end.

2. Have these events motivated you with a greater urgency to win the lost?

3. What truths in this chapter or in His Word have inspired you to a sense of urgency to evangelise?

4. Have you ever told anyone about the realities of heaven and hell? Do you believe they are necessary messages for today? Why or why not?

5. Abraham's servant, after hundreds of miles on a camel's back, refused to eat until he had shared the reason for his travel. Can you recall ever being so consumed with God's redemptive work that you forgot about food or purposely fasted for men and women to come to Christ?

6. Jesus had food to eat that the disciples did not know about. What was it? What practical things have you done that portray a sense of urgency for lost men and women?

7. Are you more food conscious or soul conscious? Why?

8. **Project** – this week:
   • fast with a sense of urgency to see people won to Christ and to break the spirit of gluttony and slothfulness;
   • share the gospel with at least one person;
   • memorise Isaiah 62:5.

   Daniel Bryant has said that 'If we live with a sense of urgency about worldwide evangelisation, it will naturally overflow toward those around us.'

Note

1. Keith Green, 'Asleep in the Light,' *Keith Green Ministry Years Vol. 1* (Brentwood: Sparrow Corp., 1987).

Chapter 16

Why You Need a Testimony (And Not a Title)

*'So he said, "**I am Abraham's servant**. The LORD has blessed my master greatly, and he has become great; and He has given Him flocks and herds, silver and gold, male and female servants, and camels and donkeys.'*
(Genesis 24:34–35)

The Bible has many examples of people who have a title, but not so many of people with true authority. You only have to think of Ahab versus Elijah, Pharaoh versus Moses, Nebuchadnezzar versus Daniel, to name just a few. I would take the power and presence of God over a title any day. And so would the apostle Paul. He saw his earthly titles as nothing compared to the all-surpassing greatness of knowing Christ (Philippians 3:8).

Paul had many titles, both from his days as a Jewish scholar and as an apostle of the Lord Jesus Christ, but he never used any of them to impress his contemporaries. Frankly, they wouldn't have been impressed if he had.

Unbelievers of our day are also singularly unimpressed with religious titles. In fact, with the recent falls of TV evangelists and preachers, you are probably better off without one. Often, when people meet someone with a title, they find it hard to identify with what the person is saying and express such excuses as, 'Well, you're a preacher. God will not work that way for me.' You need a testimony not a title.

The Bible has much to say about the value of our testimony.

1. **Those with a testimony of Jesus Christ will go to heaven, those with only a title will not** (Revelation 19:10; Hebrews 11:5). A person can say he was a deacon, led the choir, was district overseer, etc. But without a relationship with God, God will say, *'I never knew you; depart from Me'* (Matthew 7:24).

2. **Satan cannot hurt those with a testimony until their time of testifying is over** (Revelation 11:7; 2 Timothy 1:12; Philippians 1:20–25). Live boldly and confidently. God will preserve you until your time of testifying is over. No weapon formed against you will prosper.

3. **You cannot overcome Satan with a title but you do overcome with a testimony** (Revelation 12:11). Satan is not afraid of who you are, but he is afraid of the living Christ who is in you (Acts 19:15). Greater is He that is in you than he that is in the world (1 John 4:4).

4. **You cannot proclaim the gospel effectively without a testimony** (1 Corinthians 2:15; 1 Thessalonians 2:8; 2 Thessalonians 1:10). The Thessalonians believed because they saw the life of God in Paul.

5. **Most people cannot pass on their title but everyone can pass on their testimony.** Psalm 71:18 says,

    'Yes, even when I am old and gray-headed, O God, forsake me not, but keep me alive until I have declared your mighty strength to this generation, and your might and power to all that are to come.'   (Amplified Bible)

    We can pass it on to the next generation or the next-door neighbor.

The servant uses his testimony to win Laban's trust. He needs to convince Laban that he should allow his sister to go to a strange land with this mysterious traveler. After getting permission to explain why he has come, Eliezer first gives Laban some personal background about himself. He tells him whose servant he is and the orders he has been given, and testifies to how God has led him on the journey. He imparts all of this before asking for Rebekah's hand in marriage to Isaac.

The servant preempts Laban's questions by giving a testimony of the mighty work of God. He shares how God has been with his master, Abraham, and made him great (Genesis 24:35). Laban must have thought, 'If Abraham is great, how much greater must his God be?' Then Eliezer goes on to enumerate Abraham's riches, pointing to Yahweh as the great Provider, and recounts how an angel had led the way on his journey, demonstrating that God is providential. His testimony to his specific prayer for God's leading and God's specific answer immediately proves that this trip was not a scheme dreamed up in Abraham's imagination, but was led and guided supernaturally by God, witnessing to Laban that God is personal.

There is much wisdom in the servant's approach. He was not asking Laban to trust him with silver, gold, flocks or herds: he was asking for his sister. He had to win his trust quickly. Quite frankly, if I was going to trust my daughter with a stranger who had just pulled in from California, I would need to know some specifics, but more than that I would need to know it was God's supernatural leading.

When we approach unbelievers to tell them about Jesus Christ, we too are strangers looking for their hand in marriage. We have a Master whose Son is in need of a bride. How can we communicate that the person of Jesus can be trusted?

We do this by telling them how good God has been to us since we entrusted Him with our lives. In a testimony you give your personal experience of how your life has changed through your relationship with the Almighty God. Your testimony may include a number of things, miraculous healings, restored relationships, provision and growth. Whether you speak of the past or the present, your experience gives the one to whom you are speaking hope and faith that God will do the same for him or for her. All the events that make up your life can be used to identify with a myriad of people.

I grew up in a Catholic home so I have something in common with approximately 900 million people. I have brought several to a personal relationship in Jesus Christ from the Catholic faith. The first twenty-one years of my life, I was consumed with baseball. On a recent flight, I sat next to a professional baseball pitcher who was recovering from surgery on his arm. I could relate to him as I pitched in high school and college and tore a tendon in my arm that took more than a year to mend. As we talked, we found that we had common acquaintances both from the pro and college ranks, all of which made an easy transition to how my injuries had led me to a relationship with Christ.

Being open about your own life makes it possible for the other person to share about his or her personal life and needs. The Holy Spirit will then give you wisdom in how to reach out and demonstrate the reality of God's love and power.

Your testimony should have three fundamental parts: first, your life before salvation in Jesus Christ; second, the time when you put your trust in Christ's death and resurrection; third, your life now and what has happened since you trusted in Him. I would suggest having a short and a long version of your testimony so that you can *'be ready to give a defense to everyone who asks you a reason for the hope that is in you'* (1 Peter 3:15). Good instruction on testimonies, how to develop one and how to use it, can be found in the *Evangelism Explosion Workbook* by Dr James Kennedy.

Your testimony tells how you were separated from God, how you met God and how the relationship has developed. It is the story of two strangers meeting, falling in love and living happily ever after. Think of your testimony as giving an interview to a snooping news reporter or journalist who wants to know all about your relationship. Give all the details of your intimate love affair with the Bridegroom, Jesus Christ, and tell how your lover has showered you with His goodness. Your testimony is about your relationship with the person, Jesus Christ.

People will not put their trust in an abstract title. If they do, it is idolatry. We want them to put their trust in the greatest person who ever walked the earth. He has the title King of kings, but we know Him as friend. He is Lord of the

Universe, yet we get to speak with Him in His private chambers.

Your testimony enables others to transfer their trust to Jesus Christ, as Marvin Mayers highlights:

> 'Contemporary witness training does not take into account the need for such transfer of trust. The average Christian thinks that the key to witness is presenting the gospel in some form – for example, through the use of "The Four Spiritual Laws" or some equivalent approach. The key to effective witness is not directing a message at someone, rather it is the transfer of the trust bond from one's own relationship with Christ to the other person.' [1]

People are usually trusting in something for their eternal security. They have put their hope in something temporal in order to give them a personal sense of identify and security. When we appeal to them to give themselves to Jesus Christ, we are asking them to relinquish their trust in religion, in familiar ways, and in earthly securities. The question in many minds will be, 'Can your God be trusted?'

Noah built an altar after the flood (Genesis 8:20). Similarly, Joshua took twelve stones from the Jordan River, one for each tribe, to build a memorial to the Lord (Joshua 4). The altar and stone memorial were testimonies, speaking to all who passed by of who God is, what He has done and what He will do. Today, we are living stones (1 Peter 2:5). We are built up in Christ as testimonials of who He is, what He has done and what He will do. As the psalmist said,

> *'Come and hear, all you who fear God,*
> *And I will declare what He has done for my soul.'*
>
> (Psalm 66:16)

When we witness, we can point out all the reasons why the person to whom we are speaking can trust Jesus Christ. Obviously, He loved us to the point of death (John 3:16). We can share from Scripture that God is personal, that He is the Provider and that He answers prayer. However, in order for the word to be effective, it must be alive in us. The word must again take on flesh. Through his own experience, the servant demonstrated to Laban that the God whom he served was powerful, personal and providential. He showed that God was alive and working right then in their midst and could be trusted.

In his letter to the saints at Thessalonica, Paul reminded them how he had lived among them and how he had imparted not only the gospel *'but also our own souls'* (1 Thessalonians 2:8). Paul preached *'in demonstration of God's Spirit'*, so that people would put their faith in God and not human beings (1 Corinthians 2:5).

The servant approached Laban on the basis that God can be trusted. His personal testimony of God's working in both his and Abraham's life had an impact. The sense of urgency the servant displayed about his mission was a testimony of faith. It said that God is faithful. He will do what He has promised. The generous giving of fine jewelry became a demonstration of God's power, showing Laban that God is powerful, personal and at work right now. Our lives should communicate the same message to an unbelieving world. God is real. He is personal. He can be known and trusted. This is what people need to know in order to transfer their trust from the powers of darkness to the kingdom of light.

The most effective testimony is the one God is doing right now. It had to be obvious to Laban that God's hand had divinely maneuvered the events that brought the servant to his door. This is why it is so important to ask God to lead you daily to divine appointments. The director of our discipleship house, Clint Matthews, went to minister one evening at the Brazos County Jail. He prayed, asking for God's leading to those whom He had specifically prepared. Clint gave his testimony that night to a small group of prisoners. Unknown to him, one prisoner, Levon Thomas, happened to be from the same small Texas town and had attended the same high school. Levon was a few years younger and knew Clint as a popular basketball star and partygoer. Hearing how God had changed Clint's life brought Levon to repentance. After his release, he joined the discipleship house and is now discipling others. The circumstances of Levon meeting an old high school acquaintance miles apart and years later in the county jail showed Levon that God had orchestrated it. The circumstance itself was a testimony of a living God who had personally sent a messenger to him.

On one occasion I led a small band of women out to knock on doors. For many, it was their first time doing a 'cold canvas' type of evangelism and everyone was dreading it. In fact, I learned afterwards the fear was so great that some had actually prayed it would rain. Yet, each was willing to go. As we went, we prayed for divine appointments, and their dread turned into joy as God answered each woman with people open and responsive to the gospel.

The first door that I knocked on belonged to the home of a single parent whose son had played T-ball with my son. Although I had rarely talked to her during the course of the season, she let us into her home. I made a point of letting her know that God had arranged our meeting. We had chosen the neighborhood at random but God had led me to choose her door as the first one to knock on. The way it happened, we all knew that God had arranged it. Knowing the meeting was God ordained helped this woman to be open about the sin in her life and her need for the Savior.

As you recognise God working daily in the events of your life with a living testimony, your faith increases and you become more effective as a sower and reaper of the end-time harvest. What is so exciting about these appointments is that you can retrace your steps and let people know how God has divinely put this meeting together for the purpose of winning them to Himself. They can see it is not a coincidence. They witness God's power and providence first hand, and are confronted with His reality and His love reaching out to them through you. By His grace, you will lead them in an exchange of vows where they commit themselves to their eternal partner, Jesus Christ.

Study questions

1. Write out your testimony of salvation in two pages or less using the three essential elements necessary.

2. How did the servant's testimony demonstrate wisdom?

3. What did Eliezer's testimony say about God? (Read Genesis 24.)

4. What would you be able to say about your relationship with Christ that would help another transfer his or her trust to God?

5. Evaluate your various experiences and background, and tell how you could use different elements to help certain people identify with you and become receptive to you.

6. How could using your testimony help others to be honest about their relationship with God?

7. Ask God to give you an opportunity to share your testimony with an unbeliever. Write down what happens as a result.

8. We all want Jesus to return. You, perhaps, are one who has said, 'Come, Lord Jesus, come.' Yet with billions yet to know Christ this is a selfish request. If we want to hasten the return of our Lord, we need to obey the command of the Father and Son who have said 'Go.' If you were to stand before God the Father and Son would you be able to say you obeyed their command to go and bring home the bride?

Notes

1. Marvin Mayers, *Christianity Confronts Culture: A Study for Cross-Cultural Evangelism* (Grand Rapids: Zondervan, 1987), p. 23.
2. Daniel Bryant, *In the Gap* (Ventura: Regal, 1984), pp. 69–70.

Chapter 17

Holy Boldness

'Now if you will deal kindly and truly with my master, tell me.
And if not, tell me, that I may turn to the right hand,
or to the left.'
(Genesis 24:49)

After the servant's testimony, which beautifully demonstrated the awesome hand of God that led him to Rebekah,
he boldly asks for what he has come for – the bride. You may
have many friends and relatives who, through you or
through circumstances, have seen the divine intervention
of God in their lives. The purpose of God's involvement is to
bring them into the kingdom – but they must realise this and
obey. Eliezer's faith was strengthened as he shared his
testimony. It was obvious to him that God had chosen
Rebekah and was reaching out to her family. At this point,
the most unnatural thing would have been not to ask directly
for a commitment. Unfortunately, that is what so many of
us do.

So often we fail to present the gospel so that people can
obey. After seeing God's hand in the lives of our loved ones,
friends or acquaintances through healing, prevention of an
accident, or a circumstance beyond their control, we fail to
communicate that God's mercy has been reaching out to
them in order to make them part of His bride. Jesus invited
people to follow Him. We need to let them know of God's
invitation to be the bride of Christ and fellowship with Him
at the great wedding feast.

It is proper, in our culture, for a man to ask a woman for her hand in marriage. Unless the man gains the courage to 'pop the question', as we say, he stands the chance of losing the love of his life. We, the Church, are acting on behalf of the Bridegroom, Jesus Christ, and are called to seek the hand of His prospective bride. We too must have the courage to pop the question. If we lack the courage, we run the risk of losing the one Christ loves to the enemy.

After hearing of God's intervention, it was truly a question of obedience on Laban's part, as it is for all who have received a revelation of God and have heard the gospel. Paul's mission as stated in Romans 1:5 was ' ... *to call people from among all the Gentiles to the **obedience** that comes from faith'*, and he spoke of the punishment awaiting ' ... *those who do not know God, and ... those who **do not obey the gospel** of our Lord Jesus Christ'* (2 Thessalonians 1:7–8, my emphasis).

The question is obedience. *'God commands all men everywhere to repent'* (Acts 17:30). He has not invited humankind to accept His Son as Savior: He has commanded humankind to repent and serve Jesus as Lord. We are God's ambassadors. We must let people know, it is a matter of obedience.

What was it that gave Abraham's servant the boldness to enter the home of a stranger and call him to obey? First, **the servant had the right perspective** on what he had to offer to Rebekah. Perspective will give you boldness. It would be a privilege for anyone to be Isaac's bride and have a father-in-law like Abraham. This is why the servant says:

> *'Now if you will deal kindly and truly with my master, tell me. And if not, tell me, that I may turn to the right hand, or to the left.'*   (Genesis 24:49)

The servant knew that if Laban would not obey, the privilege would go to another. Isaac would have a bride.

Our perspective is much the same. We are bringing home a bride for the Lord Jesus Christ. Those who will accept, become royalty, heirs of God, joint heirs in Christ, not to mention the fact that they will miss eternity with the devil and his demons. It is a privilege to be Christ's bride. God will have His eternal companion. But those who will be blessed with this sacred union are those who are obedient by faith.

One night as I was witnessing outside a bar, three college students surrounded me and began to threaten me saying, 'How would you like your face kicked in?' I replied to them, 'You certainly have the ability to do just that if you want. But before you do, let me share this one thing. If I was out here passing out football cards and bragging about the Dallas Cowboys, you would have your arms around me buying me a beer and having a good ol' time. But, because I am passing out tracts about Jesus Christ, the Creator of the Universe, the Lord of heaven and earth, the Savior who died on the cross for your sins, you are ready to kick my face in. Do you see how wicked you are?' I was pointing my finger at them. They were stunned. Not knowing what to say apart from a few curses, they walked away. I am not recommending this method of witnessing but one of the reasons I could boldly speak to them in the face of danger was because of the perspective I had about what I was doing and whom I was serving. Paul asked for prayers from the church in Ephesus that he *'may open his mouth boldly to make known the mystery of the gospel'* (Ephesians 6:19). This is how we should declare it – boldly, without fear. When Paul wrote to the Ephesians he was in prison. He was saying to the saints at Ephesus, 'Do not let me compromise the message just because I am in prison and people may take my life.'

Whenever we compromise the gospel, the devil is having us for lunch. In other words, he is getting the best of us and winning the battle for souls. We should never lower the standard of the gospel – whether it be to save our own skin, to save our self-esteem in the face of rejection, or to fill our church buildings. Paul said,

> *'For I am not ashamed of the gospel for it is the power of God to salvation for everyone who believes; for the Jew first and also for the Greek.'* (Romans 1:17)

This can be seen in the story about the hunter and the bear: A hunter met a bear in the woods. He lifted his rifle to shoot when the bear said, 'Wait, please do not shoot. Perhaps we can talk. I know you want a fur coat and all I want is lunch. Put down the gun and let's see if we can't come to a compromise.' An hour later, the bear was sitting on a log belching from a full stomach. The hunter's gun was on the ground. The hunter was nowhere to be found. You see, they had come to a compromise. The hunter now had his fur coat and the bear had his lunch.

Not only did the servant have perspective, but **he was in the perfect will of God**. Being in God's perfect will gives us, too, the confidence to share. The servant had personally experienced Abraham's goodness and it was natural for him to share how Rebekah, in becoming Isaac's bride, would enjoy the same fellowship. As he recalled how God had providentially directed every step of his journey to Laban's house, it reinforced to him that he was in God's perfect will, and this gave him the confidence to challenge Laban to make his decision. We know it is the Lord's will to sow the seed of the gospel. We know that winning souls is wise. We know it was the last command of Jesus, and that as long as we are doing God's will, God's way, we will see God's hand which will give us the courage to proclaim the gospel fearlessly. Being in God's will means that God's Spirit specifically directs us to people He has prepared through others or through circumstances. As we sense God's direction and the presence of the Holy Spirit we are enabled to share.

The servant was also well prepared. Preparation will help us to be bold in our going. Preparation comes in the form of equipping. The servant was equipped with all his master's goods. Remember, God has loaded us down with the gifts of the Spirit. They are at our disposal as we go.

But more fundamental than his equipping with material goods was the servant's preparation through years of experience of his master Abraham. It was natural for him to share about his master and the God whom he served. And in our evangelism our first preparation is to know Jesus in order to make Him known. The young shepherd boy David knew and experienced God. When he killed the lion and the bear while protecting his sheep, his confidence in God grew giving him the courage to take on the mighty Goliath. As we experience God, we too grow in confidence. As we receive instruction and put it into practice, the Lord trains us. The best way to learn to evangelise is by doing evangelism. I believe that the only way the bride can make herself ready for the Lord's return is through witnessing. Think about the characteristics that are needed to be an effective witness. These same characteristics are what makes you His bride. They are not developed in a Sunday school class or a seminary: They are developed as we participate in our global occupation of bringing home the bride. The very act of going out refines our character making us ready for His return.

Being a witness requires that:

1. We know and love God. Evangelism deepens our love for God and our fellow humans. If we do not know God, it is unlikely we will sustain our witness very long.

2. We have the faith that overcomes fear.

3. We know God's Word and learn how to be led by the Spirit.

4. We refine our character so as not to discredit the message.

5. We learn how to pray 'Your kingdom come.' Prayer says that we humbly depend on God to give conviction, conversion, and life. We must pray for boldness.

6. We remember to be continually grateful for His saving grace in our lives.

Our determined commitment to witness throws us on absolute dependence on God. To be what we ought to be in order to share effectively, will take His presence and power working through us. In the whole process, God is sculpting us into His image, getting us ready to be His eternal partner.

The servant set apart Abraham as his master. Peter encourages us: *'in your hearts set apart Christ as Lord'* (1 Peter 3:15 NIV). Only as we set apart Christ as Lord will we be able to share Him boldly. Our sole motivation must be to see Jesus reign in every heart. If we are trying to promote our church, our ministry, our denomination, then the Spirit of God will not enable us. Paul said,

> *'...I myself always strive to have a conscience without offense toward God and men.'*   (Acts 24:16)

He had a pure motive for serving Jesus. He was not trying to prove to others he was an apostle or a Christian. He shared because Jesus was the Lord of his life. He was compelled to share out of love for Jesus. The Spirit enables those who exalt only Jesus in their hearts, to declare Him as Lord to the nations. An impure motive is one reason why evangelism is ineffective or lacking in boldness. The righteous (those who are in right relationship) will be as bold as a lion.

Setting apart Christ as Lord in your heart also means you will not fear rejection. Knowing the lordship of Jesus Christ helps us to realise people are not rejecting us as people, but our Lord. The perfect love of God will cast out such fears and free us up to share the gospel.

In order to witness **we need to be filled with the Spirit**. Paul reminded Timothy:

> *'God has not given us a spirit of fear, but of power and of love and of a sound mind.'*   (2 Timothy 1:7)

The Holy Spirit is not shy. Paul quoting the Old Testament said, *'I believed therefore I spoke'* (2 Corinthians 4:13). Believers will naturally speak about the Lord Jesus Christ. The reason the Holy Spirit is given is so that we will bear witness of our Redeemer (Acts 1:8). The apostles, after being imprisoned and given strict orders not to teach in the name of Jesus said,

> *'For we cannot but speak the things which we have seen and heard.'*   (Acts 4:20)

If you are filled with the Spirit, Jesus must spill out of your heart and through your mouth. It is from the overflow of the heart that the mouth speaks (Matthew 12:34). If Jesus is in by the Holy Spirit, He must come out. This is not for the super saints or the apostles but for all believers filled with the Holy Spirit. Acts 4:31 says,

'...and they [the believers in Jerusalem] *were all filled with the Holy Spirit, and they spoke the word of God with boldness.'*

When going out to witness, I often take my children with me. Leah, the oldest, has had the most exposure. My boldness has rubbed off on her and she is very vocal about her faith. One afternoon, while out shopping, Leah, then only seven, confronted an older gentleman at the check-out counter. She asked him, 'Do you love Jesus?' The older man, trying to placate my daughter, patted her on the head and said, 'Yes, I love Jesus.' Sensing the lack of sincerity in his answer, Leah restated, 'Do you really love Jesus?' The man could only grin in embarrassment and hope the gospel-bombardier's parents would quickly check out.

The Lord filled my young daughter with His words. He will also fill your heart to overflowing. He has loaded down your camels, and boldness is on board. You can do all things through Christ who strengthens you (Philippians 4:13). Open your mouth and allow God to fill it. Paul asked for prayer to enable him to be bold and preach the gospel without fear (Ephesians 6:19). With each step of obedience to speak about Christ, comes a greater experiential knowledge of Jesus Christ in our own lives and with it an increasing boldness to proclaim His gospel.

Study questions

1. In your opinion what is boldness? What is boldness often mistaken for? (Boldness is overcoming fear and seizing opportunities given by God to minister the gospel of Christ.)

2. Try and remember a time when an unbelieving friend or relative went through a crisis and God intervened with mercy. Did you point this out to them?

3. On a scale of 1 to 10 (10 being the highest), grade yourself as to your boldness in sharing the gospel.

4. Be honest. List the fears and hindrances that keep you from being bold.

5. Perspective is necessary to be bold. Give your perspective of what you have to offer the sinner.

6. Preparation is needed. Tell how you have been prepared and equipped for witnessing. Another means of preparation is experience. How much experience have you had in evangelism? Do you believe evangelism is the means for equipping you?

7. What is your motivation for sharing the gospel? How can experiencing the Lordship of Jesus Christ in your life liberate you to be a more effective witness?

8. What seems to be the supernatural consequence of a Spirit-filled life? What was the reason for the Holy Spirit endowment of power on the believers in Jerusalem which we read about in Acts 1:8?

9. If the apostle Paul asked for prayer to be bold, it seems the place to start is in **prayer**. **Pray** God will give you perspective. **Nurture** your relationship with God through prayer. **Ask** God to encourage and confirm what He has done in you to make you confident in Him. **Set apart** Christ as Lord of your life, giving you a clear conscience and motive for your sharing. **Pray** for the Holy Spirit to fill your life to overflowing so He may be spilled out to the world which is perishing around you.

Chapter 18

Do Not Hinder Me

'And he and the men who were with him ate and drank and stayed all night. Then they arose in the morning, and he said, "Send me away to my master." **But her brother and her mother said, "Let the young woman stay with us a few days, at least ten; after that she may go." And he said to them, "Do not hinder me,** *since the* LORD *has prospered my way; send me away so that I may go to my master."'*
(Genesis 24:54–56)

As soon as Laban agreed to give Rebekah's hand in marriage to Isaac, the servant was ready to return to his master with the bride-to-be. Laban and Rebekah's mother were startled by the servant's sense of urgency to return so quickly. The mother tried to dissuade him, asking him to give them ten more days together. What a temptation! After a long, arduous trip no one would expect this servant not to have a break before setting out on the return journey. He had deserved it.

In today's language, Laban was saying, 'What's your hurry? You've got Rebekah. Your job is as good as done. Take it easy. Relax!' The servant replied, *'Do not hinder me, since the* LORD *has prospered my way.'* The servant knew his job would not be completed until the bride was delivered to the bridegroom and nothing was going to deter him from the task. It is the same for us: **our task of evangelism will not be finished until the bride sits down with the Bridegroom at the wedding feast of the Lamb.**

It would have been so easy for this servant to consider his own desires and needs. What hinders the work of evangelism in our world today is not Communism, Humanism or Islam, but selfishness. William McDonald, in his book *True Discipleship*, points out that two out of the three men who desired to follow Jesus, in Luke 9:57–62, thought they could take care of their personal business first, as their excuses reveal. It was a case of 'me first.' As McDonald states, 'Lord ... me first are a moral absurdity and impossibility.' [1]

Selfishness kills evangelism. Since evangelism is the life-giving breath of the Church, selfishness also kills the Church. It will stifle and eventually kill the servants of evangelism as well.

> 'One day, toward the close of the Second World War in a fashionable western home, the phone rang. The woman who answered heard the words, "Hi, Mom, I'm coming home." It was her sailor son just back from active duty. He was calling from San Diego. The mother was wild with joy. Her son was alive. He went on, "I'm bringing a buddy with me. He got hurt pretty bad. Only has one eye, one arm and one leg. He has no home and I'd sure like him to live with us."
>
> The mother said, "Sure, son, he can stay with us for a while."
>
> "Mom, you do not understand. I want him to live with us always."
>
> Said the mother, "Well, OK, we'll try it for a year."
>
> "But, Mom, I want him to be with us always. He's in bad shape, one eye, one arm, one leg."
>
> The mother got impatient. "Son, you're too emotional about this. You've been in a war. He will be a drag on us."
>
> The phone clicked, and went dead. The next day the parents received a telegram from the Navy. Their son had leaped to his death from the twelfth floor of a San Diego hotel. In a few days the body was shipped home. When the casket was opened the parents stared at their son's body. He had one eye, one arm and one leg. With crushing pain came understanding. Fearing rejection,

their son had phoned seeking acceptance. His mother's unwillingness to show love and bear a burden had snapped his fragile will to live.

Selfishness is not simply unattractive. It is deadly.'[2]

Another hindrance, which has its root in selfishness, is comfort. Jesus told us we are to do one thing with self – crucify it! Without the cross, there is no Christianity. The Bible tells us to *'lay aside every weight, and the sin which so easily ensnares us'* (Hebrews 12:1). We, in the West, are ensnared by so many distractions. We are consumed by our appetite for entertainment: sports, movies, TV, video games, clubs, concerts, cruises – you name it, we have got it. The more we indulge in these things, the more we become prisoners to them until our appetite cannot be satisfied and our hunger and zeal for God in evangelism is all but dead.

Raynald III was the grossly overweight Duke of Belgium. He was nicknamed Raynald 'the fat'. After a violent quarrel, Raynald's younger brother, Edward, led a successful revolt against his fat brother and took him captive. He built a room around Raynald in the Niew Kirk Castle and promised him he could regain his title and property as soon as he was able to leave the room. This would not have been difficult for most people since the room had several windows and a door of near normal size, and none were locked or barred. The problem was Raynald's size. To regain his freedom, he needed to lose weight. But Edward knew his older brother, and each day he sent a variety of delicious foods to tempt him. Instead of dieting his way out of prison, Raynald grew fatter. When Duke Edward was accused of cruelty, he had a ready answer: 'My brother is not a prisoner. He may leave when he so wills.' Raynald stayed in the room for ten years and eventually died – a prisoner of his own appetite.

The Church has been taken captive by worldly appetites and so the work of evangelism is also held prisoner. We must throw off these things that hinder (the gods of entertainment and comfort) and pursue Christ as never before.

Douglas Hyde was a card-carrying Communist before he turned to our Lord Jesus Christ. In his book *Dedication and Leadership*, he describes a typical day as a Communist.

'Do you remember what life was really like in the Party? You got up in the morning and as you shaved you were thinking of the jobs you would do for Communism that day. You went down to breakfast and read the *Daily Worker* to get the Party line – to get the shot and shell for a fight in which you were already involved. You read every item in the paper wondering how you might be able to use it for the cause.

I had never been interested in sport but I read the sports pages in order to be able to discuss sport with others and to be able to say to them, "Have your read this in the *Daily Worker?*" I would follow this through by giving them the paper in the hope that they might turn from the sports pages and read the political ones too.

On the bus or train, on my way to work, I read the *Daily Worker* as ostentatiously as I could, holding it up so that others might read the headlines and perhaps be influenced by them. I took two copies of the paper with me; the second one I left on the seat in the hope that someone would pick it up and read it.

When I got to work, I kept the *Daily Worker* circulating. One worker after another would take it outside, read it for a few minutes and bring it back to me again. At lunchtime, in the canteen or the restaurant, I would try to start conversations with those with whom I was eating. I made a practice of sitting with different groups in order to spread my influence as widely as I could. I did not thrust Communism down their throats but steered our conversations in such a way that they could be brought round to politics or, if possible, to the campaigns which the Party was conducting at the time.

Before I left my place of work at night, there was a quick meeting of the factory group or cell. There we discussed in a few minutes the successes and failures of the day. And we discussed, too, what we hoped to be able to do on the following day.

I dashed home, had a quick meal and then went out, maybe to attend classes, maybe to be a tutor, maybe to join some Communist campaign, going from door to door canvassing or standing at the side of the road selling Communist papers – doing something for Communism. And I went home at night and dreamed of the jobs I was going to do for Communism the next day.'[3]

Here is a man that was totally committed and successfully persuading people of the values of a dead Communism. What could we achieve in Christ if our main passion was to win people to a living Savior, rather than be dominated by our own comfort? Many aspects of our life are motivated by comfort. The more things we acquire to make us comfortable, the more we are enslaved by them. The more we have, the more time is taken maintaining and repairing them. These things take our time and our money to the sacrifice of Christ's work on earth.

One other major hindrance to the work of the kingdom is our family ties. God allows the people closest to us to test our love for Him. Our earthly affections must never become more important than our work for the Master. There is nothing wrong with taking care of the family, but we must not allow family members to hinder God's purposes and selfishly put their desires ahead of God's desires, preventing us moving on in Christ.

Laban and Rebekah's mother sought to do just that. There was no need for the servant to stay any longer. The Lord's providence was obvious. It was the emotional loss of her daughter that the mother did not want to face and she was intent on delaying it as long as she could. It was for this reason that Jesus said:

> 'If anyone comes to Me and does not hate his father and mother, wife and children, brothers and sisters, yes, and his own life also, he cannot be My disciple.'   (Luke 14:33)

Our love for Jesus Christ must be supreme. He is Lord of all or not at all.

When I told my family that I was committing my life to Christ and was being baptised, they were upset and asked me not to leave the religion in which I was raised. I told them,

'Don't look at it as if I'm leaving your religion. See me as going on with Christ.' Following Jesus always means leaving something or someone behind. When I made the decision to become a full-time missionary, I faced opposition from family members again. Being a Christian is one thing, they argued, but going off to Bible college to be a priest or whatever meant I had totally flipped. I am happy to report that since that time God has changed my family and their outlook. When we made the decision to go to Nigeria, West Africa, the people that opposed us were members of the family of God. Having returned to the US having suffered hardship and sickness, our commitment to go back was resisted. 'You have such a beautiful family. How can you take five sweet kids there? What if they die?' I could lose my children to sickness but they will never be lost. As Jim Elliot, a martyred missionary to Ecuador, said, 'He is no fool who gives up what he cannot keep to gain what he cannot lose.'

This life and its comforts are not the goal. Paul said,

'For to me, to live is Christ and to die is gain.'
(Philippians 1:21)

I am so shocked to find that often when an elder's or deacon's son or daughter desires to go to foreign missions or inner-city work, their parents are the ones who object the longest and loudest. Often our motivation in bringing up our children is wanting them to know the good life, rather than giving them to Christ so that He may use them however He sees fit.

Maintain an unhindered life! Throw off the entanglements of comfort and entertainment. Say no to the worldly affections that seek to supersede Christ's love and call on your life. Rebuke the voice that says, 'Preserve this life at all cost.' *'Do not hinder me,'* said the servant whose goal was not the pleasures and comforts of this life, but pleasing his master by bringing home a bride for the Lord, Jesus Christ.

Evangelism is not finished until the bride sits down with the Bridegroom at the wedding feast of the lamb. Until then ... *'Do not hinder me.'*

Study questions

1. If you had been the servant, what do you think you would have done when asked to stay for ten days or so?

2. Though times of relaxing and refreshing are necessary, the servant does not appear to be driven by duty but compelled by love for Abraham and Isaac. His desire to see the bride in the loving arms of her bridegroom was more important to him than his fleshly desires. How does the servant's example speak to your life about your love for Christ and your sympathy towards your flesh and selfish desires?

3. In Luke 9:57-62 the two men make excuses about why they can't obey the Lord. William McDonald stated, 'Lord ... me first are a moral absurdity and impossibility.' Give an example of how selfishness kills evangelism.

4. Are there any appetites for entertainment and comforts that hinder you from doing God's will in evangelism?

5. Evaluate how your time, money and talents could be better spent to set captives free.

6. Has there been any time in your life when a relationship conflicted with God's will? Who won – the Lord or your relationship? In hindsight, what, if anything, would you do differently?

7. Have you ever hindered someone from going on in God because of personal desires for your relationship with that person? Explain.

8. Does your life portray a 'no quit' persevering attitude that says, 'Evangelism is not finished until the bride sits down with the Bridegroom at the wedding feast of the Lamb?'

Notes

1. William McDonald, *True Discipleship* (Benin City: Maranatha, 1963), p. 26.

2. Norman Lewis, *Priority One: What God Wants* (Orange: Promise, 1988), p. 110.

3. Douglas Hyde, *Dedication and Leadership* (Notre Dame: University of Notre Dame Press, 1966), pp. 22–23.

Chapter 19

Thousands of Millions

'So they sent away Rebekah their sister and her nurse,
and Abraham's servant, and his men.
And they blessed Rebekah, and said to her,
"Our sister, may you become
The mother of thousands of ten thousands;
And may your descendants possess
The gates of those who hate them."
Then Rebekah and her maids arose, and
they rode on the camels, and followed the man.
So the servant took Rebekah and departed.'
(Genesis 24:59–61)

As Rebekah left, her family blessed her, and their prophetic
words stand for all time as confirmation of God's promises to
Abraham:

> *' . . . And in you all the families of the earth shall be blessed.'*
> (Genesis 12:3b)

> *'And I will make your descendants as the dust of the earth;*
> *so that if a man could number the dust of the earth, then*
> *your descendants also could be numbered.'* (Genesis 13:16)

> *' . . . blessing I will bless you, and multiplying I will multiply*
> *your descendants as the stars of the heaven and as the sand*
> *which is on the seashore; and your descendants shall possess*
> *the gate of their enemies.'* (Genesis 22:17)

These promises made 6,000 years ago are being fulfilled today. David Barrett has documented that 'from 1968–1988, over 268 million people came to know Jesus Christ as Lord and Savior. The majority of those took place outside western Europe and the US.'[1] Jesus will have His Church. We do not have to wait for the harvest: the harvest is here. Bring out the sickle of God's Word, swing it by the power of the Holy Spirit and reap.

The Lord is building the New Jerusalem (Psalm 147:2) and in His Father's house are many mansions (John 14:2). God's 'many' equals *'thousands of ten thousands.'* He had promised that Abraham's descendants would not be able to be numbered and in Revelation the apostle John is given a revelation of the great heavenly throng of believers around the throne. It is an awesome sight, so awesome that it overwhelms him. Around the throne there are **thousands of millions**:

> *'After these things I looked, and behold, a great multitude which no one could number, of all nations, tribes, peoples and tongues, standing before the throne and before the Lamb...'* (Revelation 7:9)

Caught up in the heavenly places, John sees the reality of the promise.

We are living in this reality today as we reap the end-time harvest. What motivates us in a dark world is our hope of victory – a victory made certain by our Lord Jesus Christ. The servant was confident because he was on a mission that God Himself had promised was going to succeed. Abraham had assured him:

> *'The LORD God of heaven, who took me from my father's house, and from the land of my family, and who spoke to me and swore to me, saying, "To your descendants I give this land," He will send His angel before you, and you shall take a wife for my son from there.'* (Genesis 24:7)

Just as the angel would guarantee that he would find a wife for the master's son, so Jesus assures us, 'I will build My Church...'

The second half of the blessing, *'And may your descendants possess the gates of those who hate them',* bears a striking correlation with what Jesus said about His triumphant Church:

> *'. . . I will build My church and the gates of Hades shall not prevail against it.'*   (Matthew 16:18)

The Church will prevail against the gates of hell. As Reinhard Bonnke has said, we are 'plundering hell to populate heaven.' These scriptures are being fulfilled as the plundering is taking place as never before. We are speedily coming to the close of the earth's history as the harvest is being reaped.

Today Christianity is growing three times faster than the world's population. Seventy per cent of world evangelisation has occurred since 1900: seventy per cent of that has occurred since the Second World War, and seventy per cent of that has occurred in the last three years. Every day, more than 178,000 people come into the kingdom of God. In communist China daily 28,000 new converts confess Him as Lord; in Africa 20,000 a day; in Latin America 35,000 a day: according to the *Reader's Digest,* in these continents entire cities are being won to Christ. In India there are more than 85 million believers. More people have turned to the Lord in Muslim Iran in the last ten years than in the previous one thousand years. As a result of the Gulf War almost entire populations of Kurdish cities have been converted. In 1991, during the annual pilgrimage to Mecca, a number of Muslim Mullahs from Nigeria were praying inside the grand Mosque when Jesus appeared to them and declared that He was the Son of God and they all were converted to Christianity. *USA Today* reported there are more Christians in Russia than in the USA. Officials say 55 per cent of all Russian teachers are professing to be Christians. [2]

God is fulfilling the prophetic word given to Rebekah that she would *'become the mother of thousands of ten thousands.'* The fullness of the Gentiles is coming in. God said through Zechariah:

> *'If it is marvelous in the eyes of the remnant of this people*
> *in these days,*
> *Will it also be marvelous in My eyes?'*   (Zechariah 8:6)

If we see the great harvest as marvelous, how much more marvelous will it be for the Lord Jesus who has waited two thousand years to sit down with His bride at the wedding feast of the Lamb? This joyful conclusion is prophesied at the end of the Song of Songs:

> *'[Joyfully the radiant bride turned to him* [Jesus], *the one altogether lovely, the chief among ten thousand to her soul, and with unconcealed eagerness to begin her life of sweet companionship with him, she answered] Make haste, my beloved, and come quickly, like a gazelle or a young hart [and take me to our waiting home]...'*
> (Song of Solomon 8:14 Amplified Bible)

Jesus Christ will have His bride. Will you be a part of this last gathering of thousands of millions before the throne of God? Will you know the reward and privilege of bringing home a bride for our Lord Jesus Christ? Victory is certain, His promises are sure. He has loaded down our camels. **If you love Him, you will obey the Father and Son's command to 'Go,' so that the Spirit and the bride may soon say, 'Come, Lord Jesus.'**

Study questions

1. Comment on the similarities between Genesis 24:60 and Matthew 16:18. How does the fact that Genesis 24:60, written 6,000 years ago, is being fulfilled in your lifetime affect you?

2. What are you inspired to do as a result of hearing about the daily harvest of thousands of millions taking place?

3. Read aloud Song of Solomon 8:14 (as it is printed in this chapter). Pray it to Jesus. Write out the thoughts that flood your mind concerning this scripture. Share them with the group.

4. How has this course of study on bringing home the bride of Christ changed your life?

Notes

1. Dow Robinson, Introduction to Missions. Liberty Theological Seminary. class tape 1, videotape.
2. Francis Frangipane, in a sermon at Aldersgate United Methodist Church, College Station, Texas on 24 April 1994.

Suggested Reading

Bright, Bill, *The Transforming Power of Fasting and Prayer* (New Life Publications, 1997).

Comfort, Ray, *Hell's Best Kept Secret* (Springdale: Whitaker, 1989).

Kennedy, James D., *Evangelism Explosion*, fourth edn (1996).

Sider, Ronald, *Rich Christians in the Age of Hunger* (Downers Grove: Inter Varsity Press, 1977).

Wagner, C. Peter, *Your Spiritual Gifts Can Help Your Church Grow* (Ventura: Regal, 1979).

Wallis, Arthur, *God's Chosen Fast* (Christian Literature Crusade, 1986).

For other book and materials by Daniel Bernard, or for speaking engagements, contact him at:

PO Box 4486
Clearwater, FL33758

Or call 1-888-561-2273

If you have enjoyed this book and would like to help us to send a copy of it and many other titles to needy pastors in the **Third World**, please write for further information or send your gift to:

Sovereign World Trust
PO Box 777, Tonbridge
Kent TN11 0ZS
United Kingdom

or to the **'Sovereign World'** distributor in your country.

Visit our website at **www.sovereign-world.org**
for a full range of Sovereign World books.